MY POCKET
GURU

MY POCKET
GURU

FIND PEACE AMIDST THE MADNESS

Adamsmedia

AVON, MASSACHUSETTS

Published by

Adams Media, a division of F+W Media, Inc.

57 Littlefield Street, Avon, MA 02322. U.S.A.

www.adamsmedia.com

ISBN 10: 1-4405-9246-2

ISBN 13: 978-1-4405-9246-1

eISBN 10: 1-4405-9247-0

eISBN 13: 978-1-4405-9247-8

Printed in China.

10 9 8 7 6 5 4 3 2 1

Library of Congress Cataloging-in-Publication Data

My pocket guru.

   pages cm

  Includes index.

  ISBN 978-1-4405-9246-1 (fb) -- ISBN 1-4405-9246-2 (fb) -- ISBN 978-1-4405-9247-8 (ebook) -- ISBN 1-4405-9247-0

  1. Meditation. 2. Spiritual life. 3. Relaxation.

  BL627.M92 2015

  204'.35--dc23

2015022677

Contains material adapted from *The Everything® Guide to Reiki*, by Phylameana Lila Désy, copyright © 2012 by F+W Media, Inc., ISBN 10: 1-4405-2787-3, ISBN 13: 978-1-4405-2787-6; *The Everything® Guide to Chakra Healing*, by Heidi E. Spear, copyright © 2011 by F+W Media, Inc., ISBN 10: 1-4405-2584-6, ISBN 13: 978-1-4405-2584-1; *The Everything® Guide to Ayurveda*, by Heidi E. Spear, copyright © 2012 by F+W Media, Inc., ISBN 10: 1-4405-2996-5, ISBN 13: 978-1-4405-2996-2; *The Everything® Meditation Book*, by Rosemary Clark, copyright © 2003 by F+W Media, Inc., ISBN 10: 1-58062-665-3, ISBN 13: 978-1-58062-1; *The Everything® Buddhism Book, 2nd Edition*, by Arnie Kozak, copyright © 2011 by F+W Media, Inc., ISBN 10: 1-4405-1028-8, ISBN 13: 978-1-4405-1028-1; *The Everything® Law of Attraction Book*, by Meera Lester, copyright © 2008 by F+W Media, Inc., ISBN 10: 1-59869-775-7, ISBN 13: 978-1-59869-775-9; and *The Everything® Yoga Book*, by Cynthia Worby, copyright © 2002 by F+W Media, Inc., ISBN 10: 1-58062-594-0, ISBN 13: 978-1-58062-594-4.

Cover design by Frank Rivera.

Cover image © iStockphoto.com/hpkalyani.

Illustration on page 27 by Eric Andrews.

This book is available at quantity discounts for bulk purchases.

For information, please call 1-800-289-0963.

CONTENTS

INTRODUCTION

Do you find yourself feeling disconnected from others?

Are you searching for balance and inner peace?

Do you want to find some stability amid a whirlwind of changes?

If you're looking for instant calm that you can take with you wherever you go, then you're in the right place. In this book you'll find the secret to inner peace and harmony: exercises to open your mind and strengthen your body, routines you can do during your day without throwing off your schedule.

Here you'll find exercises to:

* Find stability
* Ground yourself
* Cleanse your mood
* Calm your mind
* Center your body

We've made this book small so you can easily carry it with you. Wherever you are in your day, the exercises will help you find a true path to the center. You don't need elaborate preparations. You don't even need much space. Just do the exercises and experience serenity.

The wisdom here has been tried and tested over centuries. Some of the exercises come from yoga; others are based on Buddhist practices. There are others drawn from the ancient Indian tradition of Ayurveda, the Japanese healing art of Reiki, or the time-honored methods of meditation. You'll learn to balance your chakras and employ the techniques of the Law of Attraction.

You can perform these exercises individually, or you can make them the basis of a regular routine. Do a couple when you first get up in the morning, some during the day, and a few more right before you go to bed. You'll find the moments of peace you need and be on the road to personal fulfillment.

WHERE DID THESE EXERCISES COME FROM?

Welcome. You're about to take the first steps in a vast ocean of possibilities, where a lot of what you may have believed will be swept away. That's okay. These exercises will help you relax during your busy day and find some peace and quiet.

Before we get started, though, we should take a look at where these practices got their start.

The exercises in this book are drawn from seven different disciplines:

1. Meditation
2. Buddhism
3. Yoga
4. Ayurveda
5. Reiki
6. Chakra Healing
7. The Law of Attraction

Let's go through them one at a time.

meditation

This is one of the most widespread practices in self-therapy. Although some people complain that "I don't have time to meditate," you can place this discipline at the center of your life and enjoy its benefits.

You may think of meditation as something you have to do isolated from other people and influences—ideally at the top of a high mountain with your feet folded under you. In reality, while physical conditioning does play a fundamental role in meditation, you don't have to stand on your head or contort your body to achieve balance or harmony. Natural postures, movements, and breathing are all that you need to start a meditation practice.

Nor is the meditative state removed from reality. In fact, it's just the opposite: The stresses and demands life makes on our attention remove us from the true reality, which is the meditative state.

Well, what if your outer life is so pressing that you need an escape once in a while? This is a legitimate concern and it comes up with everyone at some time. In this instance, meditation is not an escape. Rather, it's a way that we can understand why life is difficult at times and adjust our response accordingly.

Here are some words that will come up in some of the meditation exercises in this book:

* **Awareness:** Using the physical senses to enhance our perception of the present involves the faculties of hearing, seeing, body sensation, and breath.
* **Contemplation:** Using all your faculties (the senses of sight, hearing, touch, smell, taste, and conscious attention) to learn as much as possible about one idea or image allows all of our senses to become consciously involved in an experience.

* **Focus:** Placing attention on a single idea or image retrains it to that singularity when attention moves away from it.
* **Visualization:** Bringing to mind an object or scene that assists in fulfilling a specific purpose stimulates the subtle powers of the body to follow this course.

Meditation overlaps some of the other disciplines in this book. For instance, there are yoga meditations and meditations that are practiced as part of Ayurveda and Reiki. So don't be surprised if this term turns up a lot in the exercises.

yoga

Like meditation, yoga has been around a very long time, and, also like meditation, there are a number of common misunderstandings about it. People have been practicing yoga for almost 5,000 years, and for good reason—it works.

Yoga is an ancient art and science from India, originally designed to strengthen and align the body and quiet and focus the mind for meditation. It has been successfully adapted to the needs and lifestyles of Westerners. Yoga is a teaching that is strongly grounded in physiological reality. Your experience of the world greatly depends upon the health of your nervous system, which is impacted by the environment, heredity, and the foods you eat. The practices of yoga strengthen and purify the nervous system so we can most clearly perceive and interact in the world in a conscious and positive manner.

The word *yoga* means "to yoke or join." In the practice of yoga, we join and integrate the mind, body, and spirit into one aligned and cohesive unit. The body is the physical manifestation of spirit. Working with the body through yoga connects you with spirit, while unraveling the emotional, physical, and mental knots that bind you and blind you from your true nature. This process allows your essence to shine through and illuminate your entire being. It is a catalyst enabling you to grow in whatever way is natural and self-affirming.

A lot of yoga depends on correct postures and breath. Through practice of these, you can reconnect your body and mind and discover your spirit. You can become whole and regain an intimate knowledge of your real Self (not the little self with needs and wants that gnaws at you all day long). Yoga is the art of listening to all parts of your Self.

Most of the yoga practiced in the West is what is known as *Hatha yoga*. Hatha yoga works with postures (known as *asanas*), breathing techniques (known as *pranayama*), conscious relaxation (known as *pratyahara* and *dharana*), and meditation (known as *dhyana*).

It helps if you have certain props available for yoga. You can get these at just about any sports store or health center.

* Sticky or nonslip mat: This is a useful prop that provides traction and grip so you can concentrate on doing the posture without worrying about slipping.
* Strap or belt: A strap has many uses; for example, stretching the hamstrings in a variety of poses, or making a "longer arm" to hold on with for shoulder opening exercises.
* Three firm cotton or wool blankets: Blankets are handy for sitting on, and for placing under knees, heads, and torsos for headstands and shoulderstands.
* Metal or wooden chair without arms: A chair is wonderful for supported and modified poses.
* Wooden or foam block or a phone book: This comes in handy in "bringing the floor to you" in many postures (for example, if you are in a standing forward bend and your hands don't reach the floor, a block placed under each hand eases the effort and stretch in the hamstring); an old phone book can be encased in strong tape (duct tape works well).
* Empty wall space: A wall is a very useful tool that reinforces correct alignment, symmetry, and balance.

Yoga has its roots in the culture of India five millennia ago and spread over the whole of the Near East and then, eventually, to the West. As such, it made contact with a number of important religious traditions. Among these is Buddhism.

BUDDHISM

Buddhism traces its roots back to the Buddha, a yogi who lived more than 2,500 years ago in northern India. His revolutionary insights have withstood the test of time, and his methods can still transform lives.

Although it's considered a religion, you don't believe in Buddhism; you practice Buddhism. In fact, you don't even need to be a "Buddhist" to practice "Buddhism." You just have to sit down and meditate.

The Buddha preached this fundamental truth: "Life is suffering." Nurtured by greed, hatred, and delusion, this suffering persists throughout the world. The cessation of suffering is called *Nirvana*.

Buddhist practice emphasizes meditation as a way of centering the soul and finding inner peace. In turn, this requires mastering the arts of breathing and sitting. These may seem very simple, but they are not.

Breathing

Breathe in through your nose and out through your nose. Breathe from your diaphragm and feel it rise and fall with your breath. Let your breathing fall naturally, in and out, in and out. Now start to count your breaths. Breathe in, breathe out, and count "one." Breathe in, breathe out, and count "two." Continue until you get to ten and begin again. If you notice that your mind has begun to wander, start counting at one again.

Acknowledge the thought and go back to the breath. You will notice how hard it is to bring the mind back to the breath. The mind can be full of unruly monkeys jumping from tree to tree. Both sitting and breathing practice helps to train them to be still.

Sitting

Try to sit still. Do not move. This may seem impossible at first, but the more you move the more you will want to move. In a number of the exercises in this book, you'll apparently be doing nothing more than sitting. But you'll quickly find that to sit mindfully requires a lot of concentration.

In virtually all Buddhist meditations, you are required to take a specific posture. Put on some comfortable clothing and take off your shoes. Sit with your legs crossed, in lotus (legs crossed with each foot on the opposite thigh) or half lotus (one foot on the opposite thigh and the other foot folded on the floor) position, if you can. Put a cushion underneath you and sit forward on it so that your knees are touching the ground. You can also put the cushion between your legs or sit on a special small bench and kneel with the majority of your weight resting on the cushion so your legs don't fall asleep. Make sure you are in a quiet space with no distractions such as television, radio, or other people who are not practicing.

Keep your spine as straight as possible and the top of your head pointed toward the ceiling. Rest your hands in your lap, palms up, with one hand cradling the other. Touch your thumbs gently together. You can also rest your hands palms up or palms down on your thighs. Your lips touch lightly and your tongue can gently touch the roof of your mouth. Make sure you are not holding tension in your shoulders or anywhere else. Your eyes can be open or closed. If open, try to relax them and loosen their focus.

If you diligently practice breathing, sitting, and posture, you'll be able to effectively meditate, both Buddhist meditations and others.

ayurveda

Ayurveda is a holistic, natural system of health, originating in India more than 5,000 years ago. Perhaps the oldest extant medical system in the world, Ayurveda's teachings are timeless. Now, when looking for natural, holistic, and safe ways to create health for themselves and their families, people in the West are interested in Ayurveda for its vast knowledge and effective treatments. Ayurveda offers remedies for illness, and is designed as a preventive medicine that supports consistent health and longevity.

Ayurveda is a complete medical system. It treats the whole person as an integrated being: body, mind, and spirit. Ayurveda is a comprehensive medical system that includes surgery, psychotherapy, pediatrics, gynecology, obstetrics, ophthalmology, geriatrics, ear/nose/throat, and general medicine. All of these branches are subsumed in the holistic practice of Ayurveda, which takes into consideration all aspects of your life, and employs a variety of healing modalities to support your health and thriving day by day, year by year.

Your Constitution, the Doshas

Ayurveda assesses your state of being and the state of the natural world in terms of three basic principles, or *doshas*. The doshas are *vata*, *pitta*, and *kapha*. Vata dosha is a combination of the elements of ether and air, pitta is a combination of fire and water, and kapha is both water and earth elements. According to Ayurveda, your personal type, your *constitution*, is described by how these doshas were set in you when you were conceived.

All the doshas and elements are a part of you. For most people one or two of the doshas are most prominent at conception, and that decides their constitution. Some people are *tridoshic*, which means their constitution is vata-pitta-kapha. Most people are what is called *dual doshic*, with two doshas sharing a higher percentage proportionally. So, the dual doshic configurations of constitutional types can be vata-pitta, vata-kapha, or pitta-kapha. To nuance a bit further, one may carry a stronger proportion of one of these so there are also these last three combinations reversed to appear as pitta-vata, kapha-vata, or kapha-pitta.

Your original constitution is called your *prakruti*. Your Ayurvedic practitioner can figure out your prakruti by pulse diagnosis, and you can learn to tell which doshas are active in you once you learn which qualities are associated with each element and how to notice them in yourself. Month to month, and even hour by hour, you may notice changes in how you feel the doshas are at work inside of you.

When you are out of balance, the relationship of vata-pitta-kapha in you is called your *vikruti*. For health, you want to be in balance, which means that the relationship of vata, pitta, kapha is balanced in you in the same way it was when you were born. Various lifestyle and dietary habits can bring you out of balance, and you will learn to be able to notice in you when that is happening and how to steer yourself back toward balance.

The Qualities in Nature

Each dosha is described as a combination of two elements, and each element is described according to its qualities. Ayurveda lists twenty observable qualities. These qualities are expressed as ten sets of opposites: hot/cold, oily/dry, rough/smooth (slimy), heavy/light, soft/hard, static/mobile, cloudy/clear, gross/subtle, slow/sharp, liquid/solid (dense). Table 1 shows how Ayurveda describes each dosha and its qualities.

TABLE 1: **The Doshas and the Qualities**

DOSHA	ASSOCIATED QUALITIES
VATA	dry, light, cold, rough, subtle, mobile, clear
PITTA	hot, sharp, light, liquid, mobile, oily
KAPHA	heavy, slow, dull, cold, oily, liquid, smooth, dense, soft, static, gross, solid

Table 1 shows what qualities are associated with what dosha. For example, "solid" is typically associated with kapha because kapha has the element of earth, which is a solid, grounding force. When you feel securely solid in your life, that is a quality of kapha in you. As you do more of the Ayurveda-based exercises in this book and start observing qualities in yourself and in nature, you will become more familiar with which qualities go with which dosha. And, as you do, it will become second nature for you to notice qualities in yourself, and associate them to particular elements.

How to Recognize the Qualities in You

The following checklists are examples of how you can begin to notice how vata, pitta, and kapha are showing up in you. These checklists are to help you start to get the idea of how to observe yourself in terms of the qualities. These brief checklists are not to be used for diagnosis. They are here to give you a sense of what kinds of behaviors and patterns you'll be observing in yourself, as you begin to understand your state of health according to the doshas.

Observing Vata

* Do you talk quickly and often?
* Do you often feel anxious?
* Are you constipated?

* Are you more comfortable seeing the big picture rather than the small details?
* Do you easily feel connected to spiritual and energetic existence?

These questions help you determine if vata is working strongly in you. Talking quickly and often and feeling anxious have the "mobile" or "movement" quality of vata. If you're constipated, that points to the dry quality of vata. And if you tend to be more comfortable seeing the larger picture in life, instead of focusing on small details, that shows the spacious/ether quality of vata. If you easily and comfortably tap in to the spiritual and creative worlds, that connection is an expression of the subtle, ethereal quality of vata.

Observing Pitta

* Are you able to effectively and efficiently complete tasks?
* Are you quick to anger?
* Are you highly critical of yourself and others?
* Are you usually hot, even when others are neutral or cold?
* Are you fanatical in your spiritual, religious, or nonreligious stance?

If you answered "yes" to any of those questions, you are noticing the signs of pitta in you. Just from this checklist, you aren't making a diagnosis or judgment about whether it's balanced in you or overactive. This checklist is introducing you to some of the ways to notice pitta.

Being able to effectively and efficiently complete tasks shows the "sharp" quality of the pitta mind and the fiery quality of pitta in action. If you are quick to anger and become critical, that points to the fiery and mobile qualities of pitta. If you are usually hot, even when others around you are not, that shows the hot qualities of pitta. And if you are fanatical in your relationship to spirit or adamant about your stance against the possibility of spirit, that also points to the fiery pitta energy.

Observing Kapha

* Do you gain weight easily and have difficulty losing it?
* Most of the year, is it hard for you to get moving?
* Are you prone to depression?
* Is your sleep heavy and long-lasting?
* Are you loyal to your friends and loved ones?

This checklist helps you acclimate to noticing the qualities of kapha. Kapha is a grounded, gross (as opposed to subtle) dosha. Being of earth, it is hard, steady, and solid. Because of this, it's a stabilizing and nurturing force of life. Ways you may notice it in you could be that you have a larger frame and gain weight easily. You may have trouble initiating movement or projects because "mobility" is a quality associated with vata and pitta, not kapha. If you're prone to depression it could be a sign of the dense and dull qualities of kapha. If your sleep is heavy and long, that shows deep and slow or lethargic qualities. And your loyalty to friends shows that solid, soft side of kapha.

Creating health in Ayurveda means creating balance. Being in balance supports your biological functions, your psychological equilibrium, and your youthful spirit.

Now let's turn to another ancient set of healing practices.

REIKI

Usui Reiki Ryoho is an ancient hands-on healing art that intentionally channels ki energies to promote balance and well-being. The term Reiki is derived from two Japanese syllables, *rei* and *ki* (pronounced "ray key"), meaning "universal life energy." Rei represents the source of this energy, and ki represents the energy's movement within and around us.

Reiki Is Energy

Reiki is the source of universal life energy, and it is also a term used to describe the healing modality that accesses and transmits that energy. Reiki as a healing instrument operates through the concept that there is an unlimited supply of universal life energy available for us to tap into.

How Reiki Enters the Body

There are different opinions about how Reiki enters the body. Some people believe it is pulled upward from the earth's grounding energies through the soles of the feet. Others believe it enters from a celestial source through the top of the head at the crown. Others feel it enters through the *tan tien*, the energy center of the body, and some feel it enters through the root chakra. Plausibly, it is a combination of all of these.

How Reiki Flows from the Body

In applying Reiki to the recipient, healing energies flow out of the practitioner's body through the palms of the hands as they touch the recipient's body. The energy flow varies in speed, depending on various factors such as the extent of the recipient's illness, degree of blockage, readiness to accept change, and so on. The source offers an unlimited supply of Reiki so that we, as facilitators of Reiki, are never depleted.

The Power of Love Energy

Because of its gentle nature, Reiki is often described as a love energy. Its infinite healing power is limited only by our self-made boundaries. If you will allow it, Reiki will offer unconditional love to the child within you.

Ki animates the body and gives life its pulse. Every living thing exists because of ki. Without ki, there is no life. When a person, animal, tree, or any living thing is in poor health, it is an indication that ki is not functioning as well as it could be. A sickly body is filled with toxins or is blocked in some way, meaning that ki is not able to flow freely. The Reiki practitioner assists the recipient by channeling ki energies into the body to help break through blockages and flush out harmful toxins.

The pulsating sensation of Reiki can be felt in all parts of your body, but especially in the palms of your hands. This is because the palms are the outlets of Reiki energy. Reiki wants to flow out of your hands and be put to good use. As soon as you place your hands on yourself, or someone else, Reiki automatically turns on.

In Tune with Your Etheric Hand

No pressure is to be applied to the body when giving Reiki. Place your hands gently on the body. However, there may be situations when your hands might feel as if they are actually sinking deeply into the body while giving Reiki. This sinking or magnetic pulling sensation happens when your hand's healing energy extends itself into the deep tissues.

Preferably, Reiki treatments are done in solitude, either in quietness or with soft music being played in the background. Including

Reiki self-treatments in an already hectic and time-squeezed schedule doesn't mean you have to sacrifice other activities that you enjoy. Your Reiki self-treatments can be incorporated into other relaxing practices that are already a part of your routine. Here are some ideas:

* Perform Reiki self-treatments while you are reclining on the couch watching television or listening to music.
* Integrate your meditation time with your Reiki treatment.
* Give yourself Reiki while soaking in a hot bubble bath.

For a summary of Reiki hand positions, see the Appendix.

CHAKRA HEALING

The seven major chakras exist in you and affect you on physical, psychological, and spiritual levels. The chakras are bright, glowing energy centers that control the flow of life-force energy. Sometimes the chakras spin too slowly, sometimes too quickly, and sometimes just right. If they are spinning just right, energy travels freely to your physical, mental, and energetic bodies. This means you are firing on all cylinders. By learning about the chakras and how to balance them, you can live your life with ease, joy, clear-headedness, love, intimacy, health, security, and whatever else your heart desires. You will notice that chakras go in and out of balance, and you can learn from them and heal with them. As you balance the chakras, you become more connected to wisdom, joy, and the force of love and appreciation that connects you to everything. These good feelings go hand in hand with good health.

Chakra healing is a type of holistic healing, connecting mind, body, and spirit (or what you may call energy, Source, or God).

If you handle too much stress and neglect your body's needs, you become run down and subject to illness. Your body is intelligent and will compensate for deficiencies in various ways, keeping you as healthy as it can, as long as it can. However, you will not sustain mental or physical health for the long term if the vital life-force energy doesn't flow through you in a balanced way. You need the chakras to be unblocked for health, youthfulness, joy, and creating the life you truly desire.

What Are Chakras?

Chakras are spinning energy centers that directly influence your well-being and how consciously and happily you create your life's path. When all of the chakras are balanced, you feel safe, creative, strong, and secure in yourself and in relationships. You are comfortable speaking your mind, and your thoughts come together with clarity and ease. You also feel connected to your intuition and the vital energy of the universe. At times, chakras become imbalanced, and there are ways to bring your deficient or excessive chakras into balance.

THE SEVEN MAJOR CHAKRAS IN THE BODY.

Muladhara

The first chakra is called the root chakra, *Muladhara* in Sanskrit. The root chakra hooks into the base of the spine, in the area called the perineum. This is the area between the genitals and the anus. The root chakra's energy connects right to the earth's energy; you can draw energy upward to revitalize you, or send energy downward to ground yourself. To visualize where the Muladhara chakra is, take a deep nourishing breath in through the nose, and imagine the breath traveling down into the perineum. While your attention is there, imagine a red glow energizing that area. Exhale through your nostrils and imagine any negative energy flowing out with the breath. Repeat this a few times, to get to know the location of your Muladhara chakra.

Svadhistana

To visualize the location of the second chakra, *Svadhistana*, turn your attention to your lower abdomen, below the navel. The root of the second chakra is said to be located in the first lumbar vertebra of the spine. Svadhistana is usually translated as "sweetness" (*svad*) or "one's own place" (*sva*). This chakra is associated with the pleasures of life: sexuality, creativity, and trust in intimate relationships. To lead your mind to where this chakra is, close your eyes, breathe in deeply through the nose, and expand the belly as you envision the breath flowing into the area below your navel. Hold the breath for a moment, picturing an orange glow while keeping your attention on this area of Svadhistana energy. Exhale slowly, drawing the belly in, expelling the air as you imagine unwanted negativity leaving the body through your nose. Repeat this a few times, strengthening your ability to visualize your Svadhistana chakra. The Svadhistana chakra is also called the sacral chakra.

Manipura

Manipura is the name of the third chakra, which is located in the solar plexus region of the body. This chakra is said to be rooted in area of the seventh and eighth thoracic vertebrae. Its name means "lustrous gem," and the chakra is often depicted as glowing yellow. To become familiar with this chakra's location, place your hand on your front body between your navel and sternum. Inhale so that your body expands into that hand, and as you inhale imagine you're inhaling a warm, yellow ribbon of light. Then exhale, releasing tension from the midsection. Repeat this visualization with breath a few times to sense the placement of your Manipura chakra.

Anahata

The fourth chakra, *Anahata,* means "unstruck." This is the heart chakra, located at the center of the chest, at the fourth thoracic vertebra. To visualize the placement of this chakra, use the three-part yogic breath. On the inhale, breathe deeply and expand the belly, and on the same inhale expand the rib cage and then the chest. As you expand the chest, imagine it filling up with a green glow. On the exhale, slowly let the breath go. Repeat this a few times, acknowledging the placement of the Anahata chakra.

Vishuddha

The fifth chakra is *Vishuddha,* or the throat chakra. *Vishuddha* means "purification." The Vishuddha is the bridge from the heart chakra to the third eye. This chakra is located just above the collarbone, at the third cervical vertebra. To drop your awareness into the placement of the Vishuddha chakra, close your eyes and imagine you have just taken a large sip of clear blue water. As it goes down your throat, it washes over the throat chakra. Imagine this for a moment, clear blue water running effortlessly down the throat where the Vishuddha chakra spins.

Ajna

The third eye chakra is sometimes called the brow chakra. In Sanskrit, it's *Ajna,* "to perceive." It is located in the space between the eyes and slightly higher than the brow line. To visualize this chakra, gently place the palms of your hands over your eyes, and pivot the hands so that the fingers of the left hand overlap the fingers of the right hand. Place your attention into that space where the hands overlap. Inhale and exhale a few times, imagining indigo-colored energy flowing into that space.

Sahasrara

Sahasrara, meaning "thousandfold," is the name of the seventh chakra, the crown chakra. It's located at the top of the head. To visualize this chakra, close your eyes, and allow your breath to come in and out of your body at its own pace. Imagine the glow of any or all of the following colors surrounding the top of your head on all sides: purple, white, and/or gold. Hold your lips in a gentle, easy smile, and continue for a few breaths to allow the glow to envelop your head.

As you learn about the chakras and practice visualizing them, it will become second nature. Your relationship to your chakras will continue to grow. What might seem foreign now will seem natural soon enough.

THE LaW OF aTTRaCTION

Modern spiritual seekers have called the Law of Attraction a recently discovered ancient secret teaching. Indeed, the law is ancient in its origins. Whether or not it was ever lost or purposefully kept secret is arguable. What is true is that through the centuries, various spiritual teachers, philosophers, and others have mentioned or discussed the Law of Attraction, although they used various other names in their teachings and writings. Today, renewed interest in the subject has catapulted the ages-old concept into mainstream popular culture while simultaneously placing it under a lens of scrutiny.

What the Law Is and Isn't

You've heard old adages such as "like attracts like," "birds of a feather flock together," "as above, so below," "what you send out comes back multiplied many times over," and "ask and ye shall receive." Consider these, and you have an idea of what the Law of Attraction is. Simply put, the Law of Attraction asserts that a person's thoughts attract objects, people, and situations and circumstances, both positive and negative, into his life.

Attraction Can Bring What You Do or Don't Want

Proponents of the Law of Attraction say that the law brings you whatever you think about most. Thoughts can become emotionally charged. When you desire something—say, a new outfit—you feel emotion each time your mind thinks about having that new dress, jacket, shoes, and handbag. You are filled with excitement at the possibility of having your desire fulfilled. You believe you can have it. You deserve it. It is coming. You consider ways to speed up getting that outfit. You might even develop a plan of action for getting the money to go shopping at the mall.

FUNDAMENTALS OF THE LAW

The Law of Attraction works in response to thoughts that have become energized. What if you deliberately focused your attention on something that you wanted to call forth in your life, something you deeply desired to manifest? Would the Law of Attraction bring it to you? The answer is yes. Always.

Be Aware of Your Thoughts

It matters not if you seek wealth, great relationships, spiritual insights, good health, a large house, a new power saw, or a cast-iron skillet. But it is important to understand that your thoughts can also attract things you do not want. Whatever you fear most and think about often or obsessively can also manifest.

For example, you may love hiking around the Mojave Desert, but your greatest fear is that someday you'll encounter a rattlesnake that you didn't see until you were right upon it. You've thought about how terrified you would be when the snake strikes at your leg or foot. Repetitive thoughts that are charged with fear can set up the experience unless you let go of them. It is better to banish such dark thoughts. Don't give up hiking in the desert. Instead, be measured, thoughtful, studied, and prudent about undertaking such a hike. Know what precautions to take in order to have a safe hike. Replace your fearful thoughts with a sure-fire belief in a higher power working through you and with you, and at all times ensuring your safety.

Let Go of the Negatives, Focus on the Positives

A thorough understanding of the fundamentals of the Law of Attraction allows us to quickly achieve our goals, get more of what we want, and avoid attracting what we do not want. With deliberate and focused application of the principles of the Law of Attraction, we can all achieve our full human potential and work together toward creating a more harmonious and just world.

Know that Anything Is Possible

At first it may seem impossible that a person could shrink his debt, acquire wealth, and grow that wealth as much as his mind could imagine. But the Law of Attraction makes anything possible. There are myriad resources to teach individuals how to get rich. Often such books offer advice about how to assess your indebtedness, develop a financial plan, imagine putting every step of the plan in place, visualize what's going to happen, and actualize the events. In this way, the person accelerates the working of the Law of Attraction. Anyone can use the Law of Attraction to change his financial status or anything else he desires. You can have the kind of life you choose. It just takes a little imagination.

THE LAW IS UNBIASED

The Law of Attraction does not judge the value or worth of your thoughts. It cares not whether they are harmful or well intentioned, nor does it value whether your thoughts arise from a particular belief system. You may eschew religion and be an atheist or agnostic, or you may be deeply religious. Knowledge and practice of a spiritual tradition (or lack of belief) doesn't concern the working of the law. What matters is how you feel about what you are thinking.

Gratitude plays a role because of how it makes you feel. For example, when you are grateful for having something, you feel good, and the thoughts of possession and the positive feelings of possession bring more of the same. The law always responds to what you focus on in your thoughts and the emotion you generate in response to those thoughts; feeling strengthens the attracting power of thought.

Deliberate Intention Takes Focus

Think of how something looks under a magnifying glass or a microscope. The subject being studied comes into crisp focus and is magnified many times. This is what you do when you work with the Law of Attraction. With deliberate intention, your thoughts necessarily become not only highly focused but more concentrated and energized. You must have the intent of receiving what you wish for and not waver in your belief that the manifestation is already in the works. Dream what may have been impossible for you before you knew about the Law of Attraction. Now you understand that anything you desire will be possible to achieve or obtain. The Law of Attraction is continually responding to whatever you are thinking and feeling.

POSITIVE OR NEGATIVE ATTRACTION

Inherent in the Law of Attraction is the power to attract and repel. Just as batteries have poles that are positive and negative and function to attract and repel, your thoughts also have that power. Have you ever met people who were so self-focused that they seemed to derive pleasure from dwelling on all the things that were going wrong in their lives? They couldn't seem to quit talking about their woes. And you would listen and agree that things seemed pretty bad for them.

Perhaps you wondered what was wrong with that person that his life had enough problems to last several lifetimes. Have you ever heard the expression "stinkin' thinkin'"? His outer life may simply be a reflection of his interior world. Knowingly or unwittingly, that person is attracting more of what he is thinking about most. And most likely, he is dwelling on everything that could go wrong or get worse.

BEGINNING BASICS

An understanding of the fundamentals of the Law of Attraction is the foundation upon which to build your house of dreams. To get started with the work of bringing into your life experience the various circumstances and things that you desire, read and practice the following list of steps. Each is simple and easy to do whenever you have a quiet moment during the day.

The Six Basic Steps of Manifesting

1. Clear the clutter, confusion, and negativity from your mind. Try deep breathing, meditation, or quiet reflection to release any doubt, conflicting ideas, or disbelief. Be calmly but intensely focused on the thing you desire to manifest.

2. Set forth the intention to manifest something. Make a mental declaration of your intent. No fuzzy thinking and weak, wishy-washy dreaming allowed. Be bold and let your mind wrap around the possibility that the thing you most want is already allocated to you by the abundant universe. Perhaps what is coming is even bigger, better, and more beautiful than your desire. Allow for that in your life.

3. Be expectant. Be ready to receive. Believe you deserve it, and it is already yours.

4. Visualize yourself having it. Feel the emotion associated with getting what you desired. Resist the temptation to question or concern yourself with how the universe rearranges itself to allow your desire to manifest. In other words, don't worry about

or question the "how" aspect of manifestation. This is where you suspend disbelief.

5. Feel and express gratitude for the blessings you already have, the gifts of the universe that the higher power makes available to you, and the power that makes each manifestation possible.

6. Repeat these steps often each day.

GET READY TO START

Now that we've considered some basics about these various disciplines, it's time to try some exercises that can help you find peace amid the madness that surrounds you. Ready. Set. *Go.*

exercise 1

SITTING MEDITATION

Everyday life continually poses challenges to our inner peace. In the midst of a stressful episode, whether at home or at work, we often long for the peaceful moments that a secluded, quiet meditation offers. But the real world doesn't offer such moments when they're most needed. We have to create them. All that's needed is the desire to stop and take action—or no action, as the case may be.

1. Adjust your clothes to make them as comfortable as possible. If you're wearing a tie, loosen it. Take off your shoes, and do anything else necessary to feel good.
2. Sit on the floor. If you can fold your legs in the lotus or half lotus, that's great. If not, find a position that works for you.
3. If your hands sweat easily, you may want to keep them open, palms up. If they get cold easily, place them downward on your lap or knees. You can also place them on your tummy, fingers interlaced.
4. Keep your eyes open or closed, depending on your preference. The eyes-open position is an ideal way to begin mediation if you've never done it before, so you don't confuse the practice initially with rest or slumber.
5. Now focus your attention. If you find yourself at a standstill at work, feeling that you've come to the end of the rope you're climbing, stop. Refresh and relax from the climb. Pause all thoughts and remind yourself that your inner peace prevails. Think of that peace as a place within you.

6. Straighten your spine and lift your chin. Focus your eyes on the ceiling or the wall.

7. Take a conscious breath, slowly and deliberately. Think of your place of peace (an ideal place in which you feel unstressed and relaxed when visualized) opening its doors as the air fills your lungs. Now exhale, appreciating the moment for allowing you to pause, and return to the work at hand.

exercise 2

WALKING MEDITATION

Whether you're walking outside your apartment or on your way to a meeting at work, you can find a moment to meditate. It doesn't take any physical preparation; instead, it's a way to refocus your mind and the healing powers within it.

1. As you walk, visualize a question or problem you're stuck on.
2. Imagine it as a labyrinth and think of yourself as walking toward the center.
3. Cultivate gratitude. With each step you take, say, "I'm grateful" with sincerity.
4. Focus on taking very slow steps. As thoughts come up, let them go.
5. Honor others. Hold in your heart loved ones who are living or not and send them your energy.

exercise 3

IMPROVE YOUR CONCENTRATION

You can perform this exercise at any point during the day when you have a moment to yourself. The Buddhist *shamatha* meditation techniques involve concentrating on one thing in particular. The benefits of single-pointed concentration are many. You can make great progress in any undertaking you choose if you have the ability to focus diligently on the task at hand.

1. Choose *one* thing to concentrate on. It can be your breathing, a particular color, or the sound of rain beating against the windows.
2. Whenever you find your attention wandering, bring it back to your point of concentration.
3. Your concentration should be firm but not forced. The more you practice this exercise, the easier it will become.
4. While performing this exercise, breathe deeply and regularly. If this is your point of concentration, time the breathing: one beat in, two beats out, and maintain this.

exercise 4

OPEN YOUR AWARENESS

As compared to single-pointed concentration, the Buddhist *vipassana* meditation—insight meditation—is a more open awareness. There are several versions of this: In the Burmese tradition, the field of awareness is limited to the body; in the Thai version, the field of awareness is open to any mental content. Choose whichever version feels right to you.

1. Sit still and calm your mind, concentrating on regular breathing.
2. Focus on your chosen field of awareness. Take it all in, observing it from different angles.
3. If your focus starts to drift, you can give the new mental content a "label." This practice is called mental noting. Stick a label on it and move back to the chosen field of awareness.

Mental Noting

Mental noting helps you to be objective with your experience and avoid self-judgment. If you notice judgment is active, such as when you are criticizing yourself for attention wandering, note this "judgment" and move your attention from judgment to the next breath.

DECLARE YOUR INTENT

A fundamental practice of the Law of Attraction is visualizing manifestation. This exercise is designed to help you bring into your life the various circumstances and things you desire.

1. Clear your mind of clutter and negativity. Focus on your breathing, keeping it deep and regular.
2. Make a mental declaration of your intent. Avoid fuzzy thinking and wishy-washy aspirations. Be bold and wrap your mind around the possibility that the thing you want is already allocated to you by the universe.
3. Be expectant. Be ready to receive. Believe you deserve it and that it is already yours.
4. Visualize having it. Feel the emotion associated with getting what you desire. Resist any temptation to question or concern yourself with how the universe rearranges itself to allow your desire to manifest.
5. Feel and express gratitude for the blessings you already have, the gifts of the universe that the higher power makes available to you, and the power that makes these manifestations possible.

exercise 6

DIRECT LOVE

The Buddha said, "You can search through the entire universe for someone who is more deserving of your love and affection than you are yourself, and that person is not to be found anywhere." In this exercise, you consciously direct your attention to the generation of loving feelings.

1. Calm yourself and clear your mind. Concentrate on deep, regular breaths.
2. Bring to mind someone who is very dear to you, someone whom you can readily access loving feelings for. You can feel how this suffuses your heart with love and a sense of openness.
3. Now direct that loving feeling in four ways:

   - May you be free from danger; may you be safe.
   - May you have happiness; may you have peace.
   - May you have physical well-being and health.
   - May you have ease of well-being; may you be free from unnecessary struggle and pain.

4. Direct these feelings toward yourself and let them wash over you and fill you.
5. Now move on to a more difficult person, perhaps someone you are angry at or someone who has harmed you in the past.

Lovingkindness

Metta (lovingkindness) practice is a curious hybrid of Buddhist and yoga practices. As in the previous exercise, you direct loving feelings both toward yourself and others, including people who have wronged you. You might be thinking this is an incredibly difficult task, but this is the real challenge of *metta*—being open and loving toward everyone, even your enemies. The Dalai Lama practices lovingkindness toward the Chinese, so you can try to be open to the difficult people in your life.

exercise 7

BECOME AWARE OF YOUR BREATH

Ki is the life force or living energy that connects to all that there is and sustains our life breath. (The Chinese refer to it as *chi*, while the Hindus call it *prana*.)

The following exercise helps to open up your ki passages.

1. Sit upright with your spine straight.
2. Open your mouth, relax your jaw, stick out your tongue, and pant like a dog.
3. Continue for several minutes. These in-and-out breaths will open up your belly and clear the ki passageways from the base of your spine to your throat's vocal chords.

exercise 8

REPLACE NEGATIVE SELF-TALK

The greatest obstacle to achieving what we want and getting what we deserve is us. Time and again we talk ourselves out of it, sending out negative vibrations throughout the universe. This is an exercise to do if you find that your affirmations are not working and something seems to be blocking your ability to attract what you want.

1. Sit quietly and clear your mind, concentrating on your breathing.
2. When your mind is calm and unburdened, review your thoughts during the past twenty-four hours.

   - How many of these thoughts were positive and affirming?
   - How many of these thoughts were negative self-talk or doubtful "reality" mode?

3. If the negative thoughts have been outweighing the positive ones, flip the equation. Strengthen your positive thoughts, making them as specific as possible.

Deflecting Doubt

Affirming the belief that your desire is coming to you is the best way to deflect doubt when it creeps in. Trust that what you want is on its way, and give thanks for that.

exercise 9

SOOTHE YOUR NERVES

Essential in yoga (as well as many other disciplines) is the relaxation of the mind and body. Yoga achieves this through the posture called *savasana*. This posture also helps prepare you for breathing techniques.

1. Lie down on your back with your legs extended.
2. Turn your palms up while rotating your upper arms outward. Have your arms rest slightly away from the sides of your body.
3. Use a folded blanket under your head and neck so your forehead and chin are level with each other.
4. Balance the sides of the body, arms, and legs, feeling equal weight on the shoulders, buttocks, arms, and legs. Then release the effort.
5. Scan your body and become aware of how you feel. Note the quality of your breath as it becomes smooth and even.
6. Soften your eyes. Spread and soften your forehead skin. Feel the heaviness of the front of your brain, full of noisy thoughts. Soften and release the front of the brain toward the back of the brain.
7. Soften your ears and relax the eardrums. Relax behind your cheek muscles. Spread and soften your chin. Relax the throat muscles and soften the tongue.
8. Observe the heaviness of your body, arms, and legs as the body begins to relax and let go. Soften the diaphragm and ribs. Soften your abdomen and release your lower back to the floor.

9. Remain in savasana anywhere from five to twenty minutes. Then deepen your next exhalation and lengthen the following inhalation. Move your fingers and toes, and stretch your arms above your head. Bend your knees and slowly roll onto your right side, and use your hands and arms to come to a seated position.

exercise 10

CREATE A SACRED SPACE

Sacred space is a way of designating your meditation time as separate from the rest of your day. It doesn't have to be a literal place that you never use for anything else. Sacred space can be an energetic feeling that now is sacred time.

1. To create an actual, physical space, find somewhere that is free from distractions (a corner, a room, a place outdoors).
2. If possible, keep all of your equipment there that you use for meditation exercises. This might include a cushion, candles, a blanket, photos, or other props to help some of your meditations, and so on.
3. Since during many of these exercises you become vulnerable, pick a place in which you feel safe and secure. This includes both physical and mental challenges that may affect you.
4. When you first enter the sacred space, whether physical or mental, do a self check. How is your body feeling? Can you detect which chakras may be out of balance?
5. Taking time to sense how you are feeling physically, emotionally, mentally, and energetically gives a fuller picture of how you really are right now. When you notice how you feel, it can help you know what to balance in your energy centers so you feel even better and create health and vitality.

exercise 11

BREATHE CALMLY

One of the most well-known breathing techniques for producing a calm and steady breath pattern is *Nadi Shodhana,* an alternate nostril, channel purifying, and balancing breath. To do this, breathe in through one nostril, and exhale out the other. Then, inhale through that side and exhale out the first.

1. Sit comfortably with the spine straight.
2. Hold your right hand in *Vishnu mudra* (a hand position where the thumb, ring finger, and pinky are extended, and the other fingers are bent).
3. Close off the right nostril with the right thumb.
4. Softly breathe in through the left nostril.
5. At the top of that breath, close off the left nostril with the right ring finger and exhale through the right nostril.
6. At the bottom of that exhale, breathe back in the right nostril.
7. At the top of that inhale, close off the right nostril with the right thumb and exhale out the left nostril.
8. Repeat this pattern for a minute or two, keeping the breath soft, regular, and steady, and the shoulders relaxed.

The Nadis

Nadis are the energy channels of the body that provide the "vehicle" for the flow of prana (life force) and consciousness throughout the entire body. The central Nadi is called the *Sushumna,* which runs from the base or root of the spinal column (Muladhara chakra) to the crown of the head (Sahasrara chakra). Two other important Nadis, the *Ida* and *Pingala* begin at the base of the spine, crisscross over and around the Sushumna, and end up together in the nostrils.

exercise 12

GET IN TOUCH WITH
THE EARTH

The point of this exercise is to put you more in touch with the earth and to draw upon its positive energies. Despite what you're visualizing, you can perform this exercise anywhere.

1. Sit or lie down and clear your mind, concentrating on regular breathing.
2. Imagine you are barefoot, sitting on a stone bench alongside a grassy hillside. Focus on your feet. They are touching the ground beneath you. Imagine roots shooting out from the soles of your feet and your toes. Imagine the roots spreading wider and deeper into the soil.
3. Your feet have now sunk into the moist dirt. Wiggle your toes in your comfortable earthy slippers. Notice your ankles being tickled by the tall grasses blowing in a gentle wind. Feel the blood pumping through the veins in your legs.
4. Feel your buttocks planted firmly on the cool stone bench. Move your hips slightly from side to side, allowing your body to adjust to the natural curvature of the stone. You are now a part of this stone. You are feeling very relaxed.
5. Relax your breathing. The deeper you breathe, the more relaxed you feel. Continue to take slow, deep breaths. Listen to the constant pulse of your heartbeat. Let the sound of the steady beat of your heart drop to your solar plexus.
6. Release any tension in your back. Allow your torso to slump slightly. Every movement you make releases more and more tension from your body. Move your shoulders slightly forward. Allow your head to wobble gently from side to side. Tip your

head to the right. Now tip it to the left. Drop your chin to your chest. Allow your head to bob up and down slowly. Allow your head to wobble naturally, with no jerky motions.

7. Lift your head. Close your eyes. Focus on your eyelids. Notice the flutter of your lashes against the soft tissues under your eyes. Keeping your eyes shut, allow yourself to notice the movements of your eyeballs.

8. Take your hands and allow your fingers to walk across your scalp and through your hair. Imagine that this tingling sensation is awakening your brain and stimulating your thought processes. Comb your hair with your fingers, clearing away any debris from your aura that is obstructing your crown chakra. By doing this you are clearing a pathway for you to feed from the universe's unlimited healing energies. With your feet planted deeply into the earth, open your crown to receive the white light pouring down through your crown chakra and into your whole being. You are now aligned with the Creator.

exercise 13

ELEVATE YOUR MOOD

This exercise is based on a kind of yoga breathing that is called *Kapalabhati pranayama*, or "shining-face breathing." It makes your face luminous and glowing. As well, it is exhilarating and energizing.

1. Sit and exhale your breath completely.
2. Inhale and then exhale forcefully as if you are blowing out candles with your nostril breath. Do this ten to twenty times, quickly, depending on your stamina and comfort. The forceful exhalation will draw the abdomen into your body and will cause a spontaneous inhalation.
3. It's helpful, in the beginning, to place your palms lightly on your lower belly. Then you can feel the lower abdominal area contract upon exhalation, moving away from the palms.

IMPROVE BALANCE AND COORDINATION

This exercise, called *Parsvottanasana*, is an asymmetrical forward bend, which stretches each side of the body separately. Your chest receives an immense stretch.

1. Stand with your feet together and your arms by your sides, looking straight ahead. Then move your feet three and a half to four feet apart.
2. Place your hands on your hips. Turn your left foot in 45° to 60° and turn your right leg out.
3. Inhale, grounding your feet, lifting the arches, and bringing the inhalation and extension all the way up the legs and the body.
4. Exhale and turn to face your right leg. Place your hands palm to palm in reverse prayer position behind your middle back. Revolve your left leg in its socket, turning the front thigh to face forward (don't force or strain it).
5. Inhale and extend your spine so you are looking up. Exhale and, bending from the hips, swing your body over the right leg. Gaze at your toes.
6. See if you can balance the forward action of the torso extending over the front leg by pulling your hips back and drawing the top of the thighs and hamstrings up behind you. Then you'll be moving in two directions, creating space throughout your spine. Bend as deeply in the hips as you can, bringing your head toward your shin.
7. Stay in this pose for a few breaths and then come back up by pressing strongly into the feet. Repeat on the other side.

exercise 15

CONTROL YOUR BREATHING

This exercise, drawn from the discipline of Ayurveda, is called Three-Part Breath and is good for all doshas. When done with a focus on long, relaxed exhalations, it is especially good for calming the mind and nervous system. Avoid this exercise if you have had recent surgery or injury in your torso or head.

1. Sit comfortably with a long spine.
2. Seal your lips and relax your forehead, jaw, and belly.
3. Begin to take steady, long breaths in and out through your nostrils.
4. Let your breath slow down so much that you can feel your belly, rib cage, then chest expand and contract with each inhalation and exhalation.
5. Take a few minutes to establish a relaxed and even breathing rhythm.
6. Next, begin to slow down and extend your exhalations, allowing them to become longer than your inhalations. To help lengthen your exhalations, gently contract your abdominal muscles as you breathe out.
7. Without straining, draw your navel back to the spine to create slow-motion exhalations.
8. Gradually build your exhalations to last twice as long as your inhalations. Stay relaxed as you gently contract your abdominal muscles to squeeze the air out of your lungs. Breathing this way helps to release strong emotions such anger, frustration, and impatience.
9. Continue for three to five minutes.

exercise 16

FLOAT ON THE OCEAN

We humans have a natural affinity for water. During a busy day, this exercise can remind you of our roots in the ocean, and soothe your chaotic mind. You can perform it sitting or standing anywhere.

1. Close your eyes and breathe deeply and regularly, concentrating on your breathing, emptying your mind of all other thoughts.
2. Now imagine that you are lying inside a glass-bottomed boat that is floating over the deep blue ocean waters. You are lying on your belly, looking down toward the ocean floor. There are many colorful fish swimming in the water beneath you.
3. You are safe in the boat, yet you feel as if you are very much a part of the marine life—the coral reefs, seaweed, fish, and sea turtles. You can feel the boat rocking gently to the rhythmic motion of the ocean waves.
4. A school of dolphins now appears. As they are swimming along playfully, they begin to breach the water near the boat, splashing salty water onto the deck.
5. You are now wet and laughing. You slip out of the boat and are now swimming among the carefree dolphins.
6. Any worries or concerns you have are fading away quickly as you immerse yourself totally into the fluidity of the ocean. You are filled with joy and peace, reveling in the moment. You are now floating on top of the water, looking up at the sky and basking in the feel of the sun on your skin.
7. Slowly bring yourself back to shore, resting your hands on your lap. Open your eyes and enjoy the sights, sounds, and smells around you.

SOAK UP HEALING RAYS

The sun is a source of power and the reason our planet can support life. Many ancient religions were based on sun worship. On a sunny day, you can find calm and peace through the warmth of the sun. The sun is a natural healer and will vitalize your body, fend off depression, and keep your energy balanced. If you live in a region where sunshine is sparse, you can substitute light therapy by sitting under special lamps designed for this purpose.

1. Before your day begins and your mind becomes filled with to-do lists and responsibilities, sit by a sunny window and soak up some healing rays for a few minutes.
2. As you do so, close your eyes and concentrate on your breathing. Imagine the sun surrounding you, cradling you in its warmth and energy.
3. Let the warmth suffuse you and extend through all your limbs. Draw power from it and feel it pulsing through you with each breath you take. Offer gratitude to it for giving you the energy to get through the coming day.

COOL YOURSELF
WITH THE MOON

This breathing pattern, called Lunar Breath, helps to expel excess pitta. By directing the breath through the left nostril, which is associated with the cooling energy of the moon, the mind and body become soothed and relaxed. If you suffer from low blood pressure, depression, colds, flu, or any other respiratory conditions, avoid this pranayama.

1. Sit comfortably with a long spine.
2. Hold up your right hand and fold your index and middle fingers into the palm of your hand, keeping the thumb, ring finger, and pinky extended.
3. Seal your right nostril with your thumb and take a slow and complete breath in through your left nostril.
4. Seal your left nostril with your ring finger, release your thumb, and exhale out of the right nostril.
5. Repeat this sequence—inhaling through your left nostril and exhaling through your right.
6. Continue for three to five minutes.

MASSAGE YOUR HEART

Because this rhythmic standing spinal twist focuses on twisting the upper spine (while the hips remain stationary), it is a great way to massage and energize the heart and lungs, break up stagnation in the chest, and rebalance the nervous system. Those with spinal issues such as herniated discs or sacroiliac problems should avoid this pose.

1. Stand with your feet parallel, shoulder-width apart. Relax your arms by your sides. Soften your knees.
2. Exhale as you slowly draw your navel back toward your spine and rotate from the waist, turning your rib cage and shoulders to the left. Keep your pelvis stationary and feet flat on the floor. As you do this, bend your elbows and bring your right hand to your left shoulder and your left arm behind your back. Look over your left shoulder.
3. Inhale and sweep through center.
4. Exhale and twist to the right side. Let your arms be soft and relaxed as you twist, so one hand taps the front of your shoulder and the back of the other taps your lower back.
5. Create a steady rhythm as you rotate from side to side, coordinating your breath with your movements. Keep your spine relaxed and tall as you move. Stay focused on strong exhalations and pick up the pace to a comfortable, steady pace.
6. After ten to thirty repetitions, gradually slow the movement down until you return to stillness.
7. Pause and relax for a few breaths. Direct your awareness inside to observe and absorb the effects of the twist.

INSPIRE YOURSELF

One of the effects of a chaotic life can be bouts of depression. This simple yoga exercise helps you when you're feeling down.

1. Sit cross-legged on the floor, cupping the fingertips by your hips, and lightly lift your buttocks, stretching your torso up. Lower your buttocks back down to the floor while maintaining the life and length of the sides of the body.
2. Bend your elbows and place the back of your hands on top of your thighs, close to your hips. Press your buttock bones down as you lift the spine up. Release your shoulder blades down as you firm them into the back. Bring the upper back in without jutting out your front ribs.
3. Inhale and lengthen up the spine to the crown of your head. Exhale and bend your neck at the seventh cervical vertebrae (this is where the neck meets the shoulders).
4. Release your chin down and bring your chest to it. Close and soften your eyes.
5. Stay in this position for five minutes. Then lie down and relax.

PERFORM A BODY SCAN

An important way to bring yourself into the present moment is to do a body scan. The idea is to sit or lie down and place your attention on one body part at a time.

1. Lie down on your back, with your legs outstretched comfortably on the floor. Place a pillow or cushion underneath your knees. Do not put a pillow underneath your head.

2. Take a slow, deep inhale through your nose and exhale through your mouth. Let go. Feel yourself supported by the ground, by mother earth. You are held, you can let go. Pay attention to your breath flowing in and out for a few breaths.

3. Then turn your attention to your right foot. Notice your toes, relax the entire foot. Relax the right ankle. Feel your entire right leg. Relax the right leg. Notice the right side of your torso. Relax the right side of your torso. Relax the right shoulder. Relax the top of the right arm, relax the forearm. Relax the right hand, including the right fingers. Relax the entire right arm.

4. Notice your left foot. Relax the toes, relax the entire left foot. Relax the ankle. Feel your left leg. Relax the entire left leg. Draw your awareness to the left side of your torso. Relax the left side of your torso. Relax the left shoulder. Relax the top of the left arm, relax the forearm. Relax the entire left arm.

5. Relax the lower back. Relax the middle of your back. Relax the shoulder blades. Relax the neck. Relax the jaw. Relax the tongue. Relax the eyelids. Relax the temples. Relax the brow. Relax the entire head.

exercise 22

SEE

We are subjected every day to thousands, if not millions, of visual images. The sheer number means that useless images can crowd out those that can be helpful. The solution? Meditate on helpful images.

1. Select a picture, drawing, or representation of something you really enjoy. Place it where you can see all the details.
2. Focus your attention on the image. Take your time looking at its color. Notice how the light around it affects the shade, shadow, and depth of the color.
3. Now close your eyes and see those same details. Take your time to evoke in your mind all that you saw with your eyes opened.
4. Open your eyes to see if the visual image is the same as the mental image. If you notice a difference, do the exercise once more.

FOCUS YOUR ATTENTION

Breathing is key in most of these exercises. This exercise, which lowers your blood pressure and helps you concentrate your attention, is called *Ujjayii pranayama*.

1. Lie down on two blankets folded lengthwise with a folded blanket under your head and neck. Begin with normal breathing and relaxation for several breaths.
2. Exhale the breath completely without strain. Inhale slowly, allowing the breath to deepen. Feel your ribs expanding laterally and your chest lifting as the inhalation fills your lungs.
3. Inhale and then return to normal breathing for three complete breaths.
4. Exhale the breath completely. Resume the cycle of deep inhalation and normal exhalation, followed by three normal breaths. Repeat this pattern three times.

exercise 24

FILL YOURSELF WITH ENERGY

Pranayama is a powerful, ancient practice of directing energy in the body. Do this exercise on the go when you're feeling a big draggy during the day.

1. Sit or lie down in a comfortable position, with your spine supported.
2. Close your eyes or fix your gaze softly on a still object.
3. Inhale, expanding the belly area in three dimensions. Envision the breath going deep into the belly. As you do this, imagine that lower part of your entire torso expanding in three dimensions—the side and back body, as well as the front.
4. Keep inhaling, and imagine the torso expanding at the level of the rib cage.
5. Continue to inhale expanding the chest in front and behind to the shoulder blades.
6. Finally, as you exhale, allow the chest, rib cage, then belly to soften.

RELIEVE LOWER BACK PAIN

Prolonged tension during the day can lead to aches and pains, most often in the lower back, since sitting and standing puts a lot of pressure on it. Here's an exercise to relieve that pain.

1. Sit or lie with a rolled-up towel placed comfortably in the natural curve of your spine. If you lie down, also place a pillow under your knees.
2. Begin with a deep, long inhale and slow exhale, repeated several times. The inhale starts physically in the area of the Svadhistana (sacral) chakra and physically continues up to the Vishuddha (throat) chakra, though you can envision it going up to your Ajna chakra (the brow or third eye chakra).
3. As you inhale and expand the belly, envision the breath traveling down to feed the lotus at the Muladhara (root) chakra. As you continue to expand the torso on the inhale, envision the location of each chakra along the way, up to the Ajna chakra.
4. To keep your awareness on the calming effects of being in your physical body, do not envision the breath going up to the Sahasrara (crown) chakra. Keep the visualizations between the Muladhara and Ajna chakras for embodiment.

exercise 26

EASE YOUR EYES

Staring at a computer screen, something a lot of us do for many hours at a time, can be a strain on your eyes. Here's a quick exercise to help ease the ache.

1. Rub your hands together vigorously to create heat and energy.
2. Close your eyes and gently place your cupped palms over your eyes. Feel the heat. This is called palming the eyes.
3. Now open the eyes and look down, to the left, up, to the right, and down again. Do this a few times. Reverse the direction.
4. Spray rose water (a brand specifically designed for this purpose) into your eyes. This is cooling and refreshing.

exercise 27

EVALUATE YOUR RELATIONSHIPS

Those who have studied human relationships assert that on a deep subconscious level, we carry psychological patterns and wounds from previous relationships that can sabotage our current ones. These wounds may not even be ours; they may have been inherited from our parents.

1. Sit quietly reflecting on how your answers to the following questions might be impacting your current relationships. Then consider whether you desire to have someone in your life who triggers or engages in such behaviors.

   - Were family members verbally abusive? Was that tolerated in your family?
   - Did members of your family practice manipulation instead of truthful integrity as a means of winning?
   - Did the adults in your family stoically conceal their emotions? On the other hand, were they emotionally volatile?
   - Did either of your parents ever have an affair? If so, was trust ever restored?
   - Did anyone withhold love or intimacy as a means to manipulate?
   - Did someone suffer an addiction and hurt others as a result?
   - Was hitting or spanking a child acceptable punishment in your family?

2. Once you've thought through the answers to these questions, say aloud or to yourself, "I forgive you." Feel forgiveness for those who injured you emotionally and push the negative emotions they engendered away from yourself.

GROUND YOUR CHAKRA

Bringing energy down through the chakras is the path of manifestation. This is the way to bring ideas into physical form. Bringing your energy down through the chakras brings it from the imagination to physical reality. If you have a lot of vata energy it can manifest in an inability to focus, complete tasks, and stay calm. Bringing energy down in the body helps because you literally move energy down from your thinking mind into your grounded body. This will help you stay on task, reduce anxiety, and produce results.

1. Sit quietly, concentrating on your breathing.
2. Visualize your breath deeply filling up the belly, ribs, and chest. Then release, and make the exhale longer than the inhale.
3. As you breathe, imagine energy from universal consciousness and your thinking mind moving down through the throat (your truth), the heart (your connection to others), the solar plexus (your strength), the sacral chakra (your creativity), and your root (connecting you to the earth).

Warm Water Rather Than Cold

Ayurveda recommends that to stay hydrated, sip warm water throughout the day, instead of drinking big glasses of water a few times per day. Avoid cool water, since it will cool off your digestive fire. Warm water is best. Warmth helps correct vata and kapha imbalances.

SET YOUR INTENTION

Adding a chakra check in and intention-setting period to your morning is a great way to be mindful of how you want to feel during your day. Before you settle into your daily routine, take a moment to see how you are feeling, and set an intention.

1. Write your intention on a piece of paper. You can put it in your pocket, tape it to the back of your mobile phone, or tape it to the dashboard of your car. If you put it somewhere where you'll see it, then you'll have an easier time remembering it throughout your day.

2. If you are feeling ungrounded and separate from your body, sit on the floor and notice that you are held up by the earth. Or, stand tall and feel your feet firmly connected to the earth. Then, say to yourself, "All day I am safe, stable, and connected." Feel the support of the earth underneath you.

3. Repeat the intention three times, with your eyes closed, envisioning it to be true. As you envision it as true, you are creating that reality. If you think you'll be anxious all day, then it would be hard for you to feel otherwise.

4. When you notice an imbalance in your psychology or physical body in the morning, ask yourself which chakra that connects to, then set your intention in a way that supports that chakra's function.

BRING LIFE FORCE INTO YOUR BODY

This exercise, called the *prana mudra,* is designed to help bring life force into the body, and like the earth mudra it is connected to the Muladhara (root) chakra. These options for bringing energy to the root chakra are essential because none of the other chakras can function in sustained health if the root is not balanced.

1. Hold both hands so that the palms face up.
2. Curl the ring finger and pinky finger of each hand to touch the tip of the thumb of the same hand.
3. Keep the pointer and middle fingers straight.
4. Hold this for fifteen minutes three times a day.

As you practice hand mudras, remember to breathe. Sometimes when trying a new posture you will concentrate on getting it right, and you may hold your breath. If you find this to be so, simply return your attention to your breathing.

DEVELOP A MORNING ROUTINE

Ayurveda has a morning routine that takes care of mind, body, and sense organs. Once you start your day with this, you'll feel new energy and purpose.

1. Use a tongue scraper to clear undigested waste from your mouth.
2. Use a neti pot to clear your nasal passages.
3. Use nasal oil to keep the nasal passages moist, creating less inviting conditions for bacteria or allergens.
4. Put an Ayurvedic ear oil in your ears to keep them healthy.
5. Spray rosewater in your eyes to stop them from burning or itching.
6. Massage your entire body with oil. This will lubricate the skin, joints, and organs, stimulate lymph and blood flow for immunity, and ground your mind and body.
7. Drink a glass of warm water.
8. Take a long walk.
9. Do some of the breathing exercises found in this book.

exercise 32

HEAR

Modern life is full of noise—from the insistent electronic sounds of our computers and smartphones to the beeping of a microwave oven to the roar of traffic on city streets. Rather than try to block out all sound (which is unnatural and can trigger negative episodes), through this meditation you can determine how much sound you want to hear.

1. In your most comfortable meditation posture, close your eyes. Begin to listen.
2. Start with the farthest sounds you can identify. For example, if you hear water running from a faucet down the hallway, listen to it to the exclusion of all else. The goal is to hear *only* the running faucet and nothing else.
3. Now go to the next sound that presents itself nearer to you. For instance, if you hear the wind blowing against the window of the room you're in, listen to it and exclude everything else.
4. Continue listening to sounds that are ever closer to you. Conclude with the sounds of your breath and your heartbeat.
5. Open your eyes and renew your listening to the sounds of your everyday life.

WRITE A HAIKU

A haiku is a three-line poem that many people use as meditation aids. They can also just be a lot of fun to compose.

1. To write a haiku in English, concentrate more on simply capturing a fleeting moment, evoking a beautiful image of the ephemeral quality of life.

2. A haiku often captures a moment in nature, and typically includes a word that lets the reader know what season it is. For example, the word *daffodils* would indicate spring.

3. When you start writing haiku in English usually it's best to use two or three syllables in the first line, five in the second, and three in the last line. Three lines are common. Read several haiku first, so you can get a sense for how they feel.

4. It's traditional in Japanese haiku to use a *kireji*, or a *cutting* word. This word is used to show juxtaposition between two ideas in the haiku, or to signal the end of one of the images. In English, it's typically done with a punctuation mark, like a dash or period, since our language works differently.

5. Read your haikus to family and friends. Post them around your office at work or in your home. Use them as a focus during your meditation exercises.

exercise 34

RESPECT YOUR BODY

This yoga pose is sometimes called the warrior pose, or the *Virabhadrasana* pose, creating strength of body and mind.

1. Stand straight and extend both arms from the sides of your body. Keep your chest lifted and expanded throughout the pose.
2. Turn the left foot in 15 degrees and the right foot out 90 degrees. Exhale fully and bring the right knee over the ankle. The hip, knee, and ankle bend to achieve this.
3. Continue to extend the arms while avoiding undue pressure on the right knee. Fight against the tendency for your body to lean toward it.
4. Gaze toward your right hand and hold the pose for several breaths. To come out of it, press down on the right knee and straighten the leg, turning the foot back inward. Repeat on the other side.

exercise 35

DO A FIVE-MINUTE CHECK IN

Sometimes you just need to stop everything and do a quick mental inventory of yourself. This exercise is especially helpful if your day is more than usually chaotic. But it can also become the basis of a regular daily routine.

1. Log off of the computer.
2. Turn off your cell phone.
3. Sit down, and sit up straight. Place your feet firmly on the floor. Roll your shoulders up, back, and down.
4. Close your eyes.
5. Notice your breath. Is it shallow, short, long, deep? Observe the breath, without changing it.
6. After you notice your breath, focus lightly on it.
7. Notice the mind's activity for several breaths. As thoughts come up, allow them to float by. Return your focus lightly to the breath, so you don't get caught up in your mind's activity.
8. After observing the thoughts for several breaths, take a nice deep inhale and let it out on a longer exhale.
9. Return to normal breathing, and reflect on how your thoughts were: nervous, anxious, spinning, foggy, clear, optimistic?

exercise 36

BALANCE YOUR AFTERNOON

Between 2 and 6 P.M. is, for many people, a time when the vata dosha is dominant. If this dosha is out of balance, the afternoon can become stressful and you can be in need of a break. Here are some things you can do to bring this part of your day into balance.

1. Have a cup of decaffeinated coffee or hot tea with lemon in it. Take some time getting this; don't just grab it from the office machine. Sip, don't gulp it. Vata tends to be cold, so something warming is a nice counterpart to it.

2. Weather permitting, stroll outside and take a walk around the building, breathing deeply, concentrating on the sights, sounds, and senses. Feel the grounding quality of the earth beneath your feet.

3. If you feel like a snack, try to eat foods that are good for vata. For this it's best if about 50 percent of your diet is whole grains; 20 percent protein; 20–30 percent vegetables; and 10 percent optional fruit.

FILL YOUR DAY WITH REIKI

One way of dealing with a busy schedule is to do each of the Reiki twelve hand placements for at least five minutes at different intervals throughout the day. Map out your daily activities and combine them in partnership with the different hand placements so that they are done simultaneously each day. Here is a sample schedule of interval treatments for all twelve hand placements (for diagrams of the hand placements, see the Appendix):

* Placement 1, face: Shortly after waking up in the morning and before getting out of bed.
* Placement 2, crown and top of the head: In the morning, when you take a shower (you can do this placement as you stand in the hot streaming water).
* Placement 3, back of the head: While sitting at the breakfast table, before or after you have your first meal of the day.
* Placement 4, chin and jaw line: When you get into your car to drive to work or for errands, either before you start the engine or while the engine is warming up. (After the session, you'll be able to drive to your workplace in a state of peace and tranquility.)
* Placement 5, neck, collarbone, and heart: At lunchtime. (If you are eating at a restaurant, you can do it after you've ordered and are waiting for your lunch to be served.)
* Placement 6, ribs: Midafternoon, while you are sitting at your desk or at the coffee break table.
* Placement 7, abdomen: While sitting in the car before you drive home from your workplace.

* Placement 8, pelvic bones: While you are sitting during your ten-minute meditation practice.
* Placement 9, shoulders and shoulder blades: While sitting at the kitchen table prior to preparing your evening meal.
* Placements 10, 11, and 12, midback, lower back, and sacrum: In the evening, either while you are reclining and watching television, or while relaxing in your bed before going to sleep.

exercise 38

DE-CLUTTER YOUR SPACE

Clutter suppresses and even obstructs energy flow. Stagnant or blocked energy or chi makes your life difficult. Sapped of energy, your health suffers. Stagnant energy also blocks the flow of money. It impedes the manifestation of healthy relationships. It obstructs advancements in your chosen career path. It can bring on depression and negative patterns of thought.

1. Organize a particular room or area of your home or office.
2. Tidy it, throwing away things you no longer use or need. If you haven't touched something in six months, chances are you don't need it.
3. Once that area is completed, tackle the next room and the next until the whole house or area is re-energized.
4. Use baskets (symbolizing the reeds and grasses of nature) with lids to organize objects in a room that were carried in and forgotten. Left to pile up, they begin to slow down or block the natural flow of energizing chi.

The Ancient Cycle

In *Feng Shui Living*, Sharon Stasney noted that accumulation and letting go is actually part of an ancient yin/yang cycle. The yin part of the cycle is the accumulation of items while the yang portion is the letting go of those things. In the Law of Attraction, this is akin to making space in your life for something to manifest.

exercise 39

PRACTICE THE POWER OF BREATH

An important breath is *Dirgha* breath, the three-part or yogic breath. When you do this, you welcome the breath deep into the lungs, causing the belly and ribs to expand three-dimensionally. An easy way to learn this is by lying on your back with the knees bent. Practice for one to five minutes and then evaluate the effect. You'll probably feel more grounded, calmer, awake, and clear.

Dirgha Breath

1. Place your hands on the belly, pressing down slightly to give a bit of resistance as you breathe in.
2. Inhale deeply, so that the hands rise as you breathe in.
3. Simply relax and exhale. Practice this a while. Then rest.
4. Place your hands over the sides of your ribs. As you breathe in, try to make your ribs expand outward, into your hands. Imagine your sides having fish gills as you breathe through them.
5. Place one hand on the upper chest and collarbones and the other on the back side of your shoulders, just below the neck. As you inhale, try to breathe so deeply that even these two areas expand.
6. Combine all three aspects of this breath. Breathing in, belly, side ribs, and upper chest and back expand with the movement of the breath flowing into the lungs. Breathing out, empty out. Release and let go.

TAKE A COOLING BREATH

Often during the day, especially midsummer, it's good to take a long, cooling breath and feel the cool and calm flow through your body. Cooling Breath (also known as Shitali breathing) is done by inhaling through your mouth and exhaling through your nose. This breathing practice should be done gently and without force. It is best to practice either early or late in the day, when the air is cool. Avoid this exercise if you are experiencing extreme cold or hypothermia.

1. Sit comfortably with a long spine.
2. Purse your lips, stick your tongue out, and curl it lengthwise, into the shape of a straw.
3. Inhale slowly through the straw and fill your lungs completely.
4. Relax your tongue and draw it back into your mouth, seal your lips, and exhale through your nose very slowly.
5. Repeat this cycle, inhaling though your curled tongue, closing your mouth and exhaling through your nostrils, for three to five minutes.

If you can't curl your tongue, just keep it relaxed in your mouth and inhale through pursed lips.

MEDITATE WITH MALAS

You can help focus your mind by using malas during your meditation. Malas are beads, strung on a loop, numbering 108. This is a sacred number in the yogic tradition. Malas are made of various materials, including wood, gemstones, and crystals. As you infuse them with blessings and prayers, they hold that vibration. This kind of repeated mantra meditation is called *japa*.

1. Get in a comfortable position for meditation, in a quiet spot.
2. Choose a mantra.
3. Start with the bead next to the "guru" bead, which is the bead at the knot. Hold the first bead in between your thumb and middle finger. Move the beads between those two fingers, one by one; at each bead repeat the mantra you've chosen.
4. When you've passed each bead through your fingers and you arrive at the guru bead, you've done 108 repetitions of the mantra. Do not cross over or use the guru bead. Instead, you can do another round by passing the beads between your fingers in the other direction.
5. After you've completed your japa meditation for the number of rounds you've chosen, take a few moments to stop and integrate the experience. Allow the effects of the japa to resonate within you.

SIT FOR REFRESHMENT

Today, with laptops, iPads, netbooks, and eBooks there are various options for how you will read, do your work, and stay connected. It's easy to get sucked into e-mail, Internet surfing, paper writing, and shopping online. Begin to get into the habit of paying attention to your body's needs and not getting trapped in a seated position for hours on end without a physical break. It's worth taking short breaks, because your physical condition will affect your mental condition and ability to focus and stay refreshed during a long workday or project.

1. When you sit at a desk, your feet should be on the floor or on a block so that they are at 90-degree angles.
2. Your spine should be in a neutral position with the natural curves supported. Use a back roll at your lumbar spine so you can lean back and relax if you'll be sitting off and on for a while.
3. Your arms should hang at your sides, and ideally have arm rests to rest on. Your arms should be bending in 90-degree angles as you type.
4. Your keyboard should be separate from the monitor so that the keyboard can be in a place where your arms can be bent at 90-degree angles.
5. The monitor should be high enough so it is at eye-level. You can prop it on a shoebox or yoga block if it's not high enough. Feel that this seated posture, like yoga postures, is steady and comfortable.

exercise 43

CHANGE YOUR MOOD

If you're feeling heavy and unmotivated, here's an exercise to give you a five-minute break and switch your mood.

1. Stop what you're doing (or not doing), and write down something that you'd rather be doing instead, whether it's being with your children, going to a movie, or going to the beach.
2. Make it simple, and also something you'd really like to do.
3. Now write down the steps you have to take to make it happen. Resolve to find time to do each step, as you can.

Motivational Quotes

Motivational words have a significant impact on your mood and physical health. Reading an inspiring quotation can often change your state of mind. Write a bunch of quotations you find especially moving and powerful on index cards, and put them up where you'll see them. Feel free to swap them out for new ones regularly.

exercise 44

SHAKE IT OFF

Taylor Swift is right: Sometimes you just need to shake it off and move on. This is a great, short exercise to re-center and recommit.

1. Stand up where you are and feel your feet firmly on the ground.
2. Now lift one foot at a time and shake your leg while you inhale and exhale three times. (If balancing is hard for you, hold on to the back of a chair so you don't fall.)
3. After you shake out both legs, shake out your arms for three long breaths.

Take It One Minute at a Time

Sometimes the best thing you can do is make a momentary shift in what you're doing, and that can change your mood. Of course, if your kapha energy is in excess, it will take more effort to really change your psychological and physical states in a sustained way. So just take one step at a time; "one moment at a time" is the tried-and-true method: one meal, one brisk walk, and one new adventure at a time.

exercise 45

SALUTE THE SUN!

This sequence is a great way to get yourself in a good place early in the day. It also nourishes the endocrine, circulatory, respiratory, digestive, and immune systems.

1. Stand with feet hip-width apart and parallel. Distribute the weight evenly between the balls and heels of each foot. Engage the legs and lengthen the spine. Stand tall with relaxed shoulders. Bring your palms together in front of the heart. Notice your breath. Begin taking slow, deep breaths. Use this breath to establish a steady rhythm for the sequence.
2. Inhale and raise the arms out to the sides and up overhead. Press down through the feet, lift out of the waist, and lengthen the fingertips to the sky.
3. Exhale and swan dive forward, sweeping the arms out to the sides as you hinge forward from the hips. Place your hands on the floor or your shins. If the hamstrings are tight, bend the knees a bit or use blocks as props underneath your hands. (This position is called the Standing Forward Fold.)
4. Inhale, press down through the hands and feet, look forward, and lengthen the spine, lifting up halfway into a Jackknife position (holding your body in a V position, like an unfolded jackknife).
5. Exhale and return to Standing Forward Fold, gently drawing the torso toward the thighs.
6. Bend the knees and bring the palms to the floor, framing the feet.

7. Inhale and step the left foot back into a lunge. Sweep the arms forward and overhead. The heart lifts while the shoulders and hips sink into gravity. You may wish to place the left knee on the floor to modify the lunge.

8. Exhale, sweep the palms down to the floor to frame the foot, and step the right foot back into push-up position. Breathe. To modify, bring the knees to the floor.

9. Exhale and lower to the earth, landing the hips, ribs, and chest all at the same time. Elbows stay close by the sides, fingers spread wide.

10. Plant the palms and pubic bone. Inhale and peel the forehead, chin, and chest away from the earth. Keep the elbows in toward the ribs and the shoulders relaxed.

11. Exhale, curl the toes under, press palms into the ground, and lift the hips toward the sky. Breathe deeply in this pose. Press the belly and chest back toward the thighs. Lengthen the spine from the crown of the head through the tip of the tailbone. Relax the shoulder blades down the back. Root the palms and heels down.

12. Inhale and step the left foot between the hands for lunge. You may need to reach back and help the foot step all the way forward. Arms sweep forward and overhead. Lift up through the chest and the crown. Let the shoulders and tailbone relax down. To modify the lunge, simply lower the right knee to the floor.

13. Exhale and sweep the hands to the floor, step the right foot beside the left. Place the hands alongside the feet or on the shins.

14. Inhale and look up as you lift the chest and straighten the arms and legs, coming into Jackknife. Root down through the palms and feet. Keep a long spine.

15. Exhale and release back down. Gently press the belly toward the thighs and the heart toward the shins. Bend the knees slightly if you need to.

16. Ground through the feet and legs. Inhale and sweep the arms out to the sides and overhead as you press all the way up to standing. Palms touch overhead.

17. Exhale and lower the palms down to the heart. Pause.

18. Repeat the sequence once more, leading with the right leg this time. Don't be afraid to break a sweat and challenge yourself!

19. Pause and relax. With your awareness, follow the flow of your breath, letting it gradually slow down. Tune in to the flow of energy throughout your body and mind.

PERFORM SKULL-SHINING BREATH

This is an energizing breath that cleanses the lungs and entire respiratory tract. Skull-Shining Breath (also known as *Kapalabhati*, first explored in Exercise 13 in a gentler fashion) improves digestion and metabolism, strengthens the abdominal muscles, and energizes the mind.

Because this is such a powerful pranayama, there are several contraindications. Do not practice this technique if you have any of the following conditions: pregnancy; heart conditions, including hypertension; respiratory conditions; nervous system conditions; recent surgery; inflammation in the abdominal or thoracic regions; menstruation (the first few days).

Skull-Shining Breath is done by quickly and gently contracting the abdominal muscles during your exhalation and completely relaxing them during your inhalation. This results in a rhythmic pumping of the belly by alternating short, explosive exhales (expulsions) with slightly longer, and passive, inhales. The expulsions force the air out of the lungs, creating a vacuum. The release of the abdominal muscles allow for an automatic inhale to occur as the air sucks back into the lungs to fill the vacuum.

Skull-Shining Breath

1. Sit in a comfortable position with your spine erect. Take a moment to relax your body and tune in to your breath.
2. Seal your lips, and notice your breath flowing in and out of your nostrils. Allow your breath to become steady and deep. You will be breathing through the nostrils throughout this practice.

3. Place one hand on your lower belly to help focus your attention on isolating and contracting this area.
4. Quickly contract your abdominal muscles, pushing a burst of air out of your lungs. Then release the contraction, so the belly relaxes, and allow air to passively suck back into your lungs.
5. As you repeat this, let your pace be slow and steady. Repeat fifteen times, creating a comfortable and smooth rhythm. With practice you will become more adept at contracting and releasing your belly.
6. Do one round of fifteen to thirty expulsions to start. Gradually increase to three rounds of thirty expulsions. Allow yourself to take several natural breaths in between each round to integrate the energy of the pranayama.

exercise 47

BREATHE LIKE A LION

Lion's Breath, also called *Simhasana*, prevents kapha accumulation in the body by stimulating the nerves, senses, and mind. It energizes the immune system, which can get sluggish for kapha types. It also relieves tension in the chest and strengthens the lungs, which are the home of kapha in the body. Avoid this breath if you have recent or chronic injury to the knees, face, neck, or tongue.

Lion's Breath

1. Sit in a comfortable position, either in a chair or kneeling on the floor with your hips on your heels. Ground your weight down into both sitz bones and reach the crown of the head up to lengthen the spine. Take a moment to relax your body.
2. Close your mouth and notice your breath flowing in and out of your nostrils. Allow it to become steady and rhythmic.
3. Place your hands on your thighs with your fingers fanned out.
4. Inhale deeply through your nose as you draw your belly inward and press your chest forward, arching your upper back. Lift your chin, open your eyes wide, and gaze upward at the spot between the eyebrows.
5. Open your mouth and stick out your tongue. Stretch the tip of your tongue down toward the chin, contract the epiglottis in the front of your throat (the swallowing muscles), and slowly exhale all of the breath out, while whispering a loud, strong "HAAAA" sound.
6. Repeat steps 4 and 5 four to six times. Then pause and relax. Close your eyes and let go as you feel the energy flowing through your head, eyes, throat, and belly.

DEVELOP AN EVENING ROUTINE

A regular routine in the evening can be very helpful in finding peace and calm after a long, hectic day. Try to follow these guidelines as much as possible every evening.

1. Pick a regular time for dinner and stick to it. Usually it's best to eat between 6 P.M. and 7 P.M.; this gives you time to digest your food before going to bed.
2. Around 8:30 P.M., do something calming and soothing with your friends and family or by yourself.
3. Drink a cup of warm milk before bedtime. You can add a teaspoon of ghee and a few spices such as turmeric, cardamom, and cinnamon or nutmeg.
4. Before going to bed, it's great to do a self-massage, particularly of the feet and the crown of the head. Take your time massaging the feet with warm oil, and luxuriate in the sensations as you massage your feet. Take nice, deep breaths. After massaging your feet, wash your hands with warm soapy water, and then apply oil to the crown of your head and forehead.
5. Try to get to bed by 10 P.M. to get the full eight hours of sleep your body needs to function at its best.

exercise 49

ENERGIZE YOUR INTENTION

As you work to attract good things to you, you'll find that success depends on your intention. One way to energize your intentional thought is by meditating about it.

1. Sit still and concentrate on deep, cleansing breaths.
2. Clear your mind and concentrate on setting up a powerful magnetic attraction to the object of your desire.
3. Continue to concentrate, paying attention to your breathing. Think about why you want what you want, sending out your thoughts to the universe.
4. After two or three minutes, end the meditation by thanking the universe for listening to you and for sending you what you've wished for.

Align Your Thoughts

When your thoughts, emotions, and intentions are aligned 100 percent on achieving the optimal outcome, you will experience greater success. Conversely, when you dilute your intention by permitting negative thoughts, you may fail to achieve your desired goal.

exercise 50

OXYGENATE YOUR CELLS

This exercise will relax you while sending much-needed oxygen into your blood cells. This in turn will promote energy throughout your body.

1. Lie down on two blankets folded lengthwise, with a folded blanket under your head and neck.
2. For several breaths, breathe normally and relax your body.
3. Exhale the breath completely without strain. Inhale the breath slowly, filling your lungs and lifting and expanding your chest.
4. Slowly exhale, and control the flow of breath as it leaves the body. The breath remains soft and smooth and without strain. Keep the inhalations and exhalations steady and even.
5. Continue this breath for two more complete breaths. Inhale and then return to normal breathing for three complete breaths. Exhale the breath completely.
6. Resume the cycle and repeat three more times, ending on the inhalation.

CLEANSE YOUR MIND

Walking can become a meditation if you take each step consciously and mindfully. As you walk, pay attention to the following things. When you're done with your walk, sit quietly and observe your state of mind. Do you feel clearer and calmer?

1. Observe how the heel reaches the ground before the balls of the foot.
2. Be aware of the contact between the sole of your foot and the ground.
3. Notice the texture and quality of the ground.
4. Feel the shift in weight as you transfer from one leg to the other.
5. Observe where your center of gravity is with each step you take.
6. Observe any thoughts that arise and let them flow through you without judging them.

exercise 52

FIND STABILITY

Stability can be both physical and mental. The following exercise is a yoga pose called Tree Pose. And what could be more stable than a tree? Standing poses such as this one strengthen the body, steady the mind, and build concentration.

1. Stand in Tadasana (see Exercise 63), feet hip-width apart and firmly pressing into the floor.
2. Shift your weight onto the left foot.
3. Bring the sole of the right foot to rest on the inner ankle of the left foot. The knee should point outward. Stabilize yourself; feel balanced.
4. Slide the right foot up the leg (pausing at the knee or upper inner thigh). Press your foot and leg into each other for better balance.
5. Fix your gaze on a steady point in front of you. Maintain a steady, soft gaze. Keep the breath steady and slow.
6. When you feel stable, raise the arms into a V position overhead and relax the shoulders.
7. Imagine yourself as a tree that can bend in the wind, while remaining stable and solid.
8. Hold this posture for a few more breaths, focusing the gaze and the mind.
9. To release this posture, exhale and lower the arms down to your sides. Lower the right foot to the ground.
10. Repeat this posture on the other side.

exercise 53

TOUCH

The sense of touch conveys a great deal of information that we might otherwise miss, if our sensory input was confined to the other four senses. According to yoga science, the sense of touch leads to understanding in a manner that regular learning cannot fulfill. Use this meditative technique to renew your sense of touch.

1. For this meditation, use clay, Play-Doh, or some other easily moldable material.
2. In your most comfortable meditation position, begin with your eyes open. Start with the hand you don't normally use. If you're right handed, start with your left hand.
3. Work the material slowly. Press it and notice the reaction of the material. Give this a maximum of two minutes. Notice the material's response to you pressing it, squeezing it, and turning it. (Remember that you're not trying to create something here; rather you're investigating your sense of touch.)
4. When you stop, close your eyes. Take notice of the sensations in your hand. Start from the wrist and move outward to the palm. From the palm move to each finger in turn and move outward to the tip.
5. Open your eyes and practice this exercise with your other hand. If you want to continue the exercise, concentrate on arriving at the same degree of sensitivity and awareness in each hand.

exercise 54

MASTER A MANTRA

Mantras are sounds, words, or phrases that are repeatedly recited in a conscious manner. They are used as tools for focusing during meditation. The practice of repeating the mantra, silently or audibly, is called *japa* (meaning "muttering"). Mantras are meant to be repeated thousands of times so that you become deeply absorbed in the mantra's sound.

1. Settle on a mantra. It can be a word or a phrase, but it should be affirming. The most famous mantra in Vajrayana Buddhism is *Om mani padme hum* (roughly translating to "Hail to the jewel in the Lotus"). Other Buddhist traditional mantras include *Namo Amito* ("Glory to Amitabha") and *Namu myoho renge kyo* ("Glory to the Lotus Sutra").

2. Assume a comfortable pose for meditation and begin your conscious breathing, making sure inhalation and exhalation are full and unhurried.

3. Repeat your mantra, either aloud or silently. Concentrate both on the sound of the words and their meaning.

4. Continue meditating and repeating your mantra as you feel your mind clear of debris and distractions.

LET REIKI FLOW THROUGH YOU

In the art of Reiki, it's important that the practitioners learn to feel Reiki flowing through them. You may notice your palms are generating pulsing energies, or you may sense energy fluctuations pulsing through your entire body. The following exercise will help you visualize that energy going out of the body wherever you direct it.

1. Visualize water flowing from a spigot at different velocities into a basin below it. The flow of the water is determined according to the adjustment of the spigot's knob. When the knob is shut tightly, it blocks water from running out. However, when the knob is turned in varying increments, it allows the water to drip, to trickle in a thin stream, or to gush out quickly.

2. As you place your hands, think of Reiki flowing from the palms into your body (self-treatment) or into another person's body similar to the way in which water runs from a spigot into a basin.

3. In doing self-treatments, imagine your body is the basin that needs filling, and the palms of your hands, facilitating the healing energies, represent the spigot.

REMEMBER WHAT YOU'VE FORGOTTEN

The Hakini mudra, named after the god Hakini, will help you concentrate, and also remember something you've forgotten. It is connected to the third eye chakra, where your intuition and imagination reside.

1. Hold your hands with palms facing each other, but not touching.
2. Bring the fingertips of the right hand to touch the fingertips of the left, pinky to pinky, ring finger to ring finger, etc.
3. Direct your gaze upward.
4. On the inhale place your tongue against the roof of your mouth.
5. On the exhale, allow the tongue to relax back down.
6. See if you've remembered what you temporarily forgot.

ATTRACT A HEALTHY BODY

What messages do you play over and over in your mind about your body? What the mind constantly focuses on with feeling, the subconscious tends to believe. It's important, therefore, to train your mind to visualize a healthy body so you can attract it to yourself.

1. Close your eyes and think about your body. Do you see yourself as too thin, fat, disproportionate, flabby, old, wrinkled, weak, frail, wracked with pain, or ill?
2. Now turn your thoughts to the kind of body you want to have. Be specific and detailed in your visualization.
3. Your thoughts are magnetized by feeling, so if you feel you are weak, for example, you cannot attract strength. Pick a negative characteristic you associate with your body and instead of focusing on it, push it away. If you feel you're weak, imagine yourself as strong.
4. Let your positive feelings flow through your body and mind and out into the universe.
5. Express gratitude to the universe for supplying you with what you want.

Prayer for Vibrant Health

Oh, Holy One, I appreciate the gift of my body as the vessel that carries my consciousness through life. Now, as I move my awareness deeply inward, my mind's eye examines this body from the feet to the head. I perceive it as a living mass of cells, like vibrating particles of light, each performing its function exactly as it was created to do to keep this body vibrantly healthy and strong.

The rays of thy holy light manifest through the prism of my mind as healing colors of the rainbow. I hear the cosmic vibration—OM—and feel blissfully alive and sustained.

Focusing my attention on the heart space, I enter the temple of peace. Resting in your restorative and loving presence, I give thanks.

PREPARE FOR HEALING ENERGIES

Practitioners of Reiki practice a ritual called Gassho (pronounced "gash sho"). It is used as an acknowledgment, a prayerful greeting of sorts.

1. Perform this ritual before beginning a Reiki self-healing session.
2. Stand straight and bring your hands together in a prayerlike fashion in front of your heart. In using Gassho, you are recognizing the source of the healing energies and thanking the Creator for the opportunity to serve as a vessel for Reiki to flow through.
3. Perform the Gassho ritual for a few brief seconds before the session begins and again at the end of the session. You can state out loud during the Gassho ritual the healing intention that was selected for the session.

exercise 59

STEAM WITH ESSENTIAL OILS

Especially at times of year or in climates where the air is dry, steaming with an essential oil is a fast way to get the benefits of the essential oils. The vapor infused with healing properties rises into the nasal passages, entering your system immediately. Steaming is an effective, easy, and soothing way to feel the benefits of essential oils.

1. Have a towel and your essential oil nearby.
2. Get a bowl that is approximately ten to twelve inches in diameter.
3. Boil enough water to fill the bowl one-half to two-thirds full.
4. Pour the steaming water into the bowl, and then add one drop of the essential oil to the bowl.
5. Lean your head into the flow of the steam, and put the towel over your head to cover your head and the bowl.
6. Inhale deeply through both nostrils, exhale gently through the mouth. Repeat this several times.
7. If you would like to, also close one nostril with your finger, and inhale and exhale through one nostril at a time to make sure that each side is receiving the benefits.
8. If one drop of the essential oil wasn't strong enough, or if the scent diminishes, add another drop. It's doubtful you will need more than two drops of the essential oil.
9. When you are finished steaming, sit down. Take a moment to notice the effects. Practice this two to three times per day if you're working with a particular imbalance or onset of a cold.

DRIVE MINDFULLY

Most of us spend large parts of our lives sitting in cars—driving to and from work, school, the store, and so on. Here are ways you can be more mindful about the act of sitting in the car while you're driving.

1. When getting into the car, turn so your back is toward the seat. Engage your abdomen and push your hips back so you slowly sit down into the chair.
2. Once you're in the chair, pivot your body so your back is against the back of the car seat and your feet are toward the pedals.
3. Get a back roll (you can buy one at a back-care store) or roll up a towel. Put it in the natural curve of your lumbar spine. Lean back. You want to feel as if your spine is supported, with its natural curves. When you have the back roll in the correct spot, you will notice the difference.
4. Once you're seated and your back feels supported, place your hands on the wheel. Make sure you don't have far to reach so you can bend your arms.
5. If you're driving more than fifteen minutes, practice some slight pelvic tilts while driving. Also, while paying close attention to driving, take one hand off the wheel at a time and wiggle the fingers; shake the arm a little.
6. To exit the car, reverse the way you got into it.

TAKE A BREAK

Even if you have excellent posture at your desk, sitting in one place too long can lead to tension and aches and pains. Take breaks to roll your shoulders.

1. Gently turn your head to look side to side. Rub your hands together to generate heat, then palm your eyes with your cupped hands and breath deeply to relax.
2. Stand up at least every half hour to move your limbs before sitting back down.
3. Use this time to check on your chakras. Keep crystals in your desk and when you notice a certain deficiency that you want to boost, hold the crystal in your hands for a few moments and visualize its energizing power.
4. Make color-infused water the night before, using a few drops of food coloring, and sip the colored water throughout your day at work.
5. Bring an object into work that is the color of the chakra you are working on. Throughout your day, look at the object taking in the color's vibrations.
6. Have photographs with you of loved ones, to keep your heart chakra strong.

PERFORM THE SO HUM MEDITATION

One of the simplest and most profound mantras is *So Hum*—"I am that I am." Meditating on this simple phrase, you penetrate your layers of protection and self-criticism. As you repeat So Hum over and over, you bring your awareness to who you are at the core; the quiet, still place. You discover simply that you exist, that you are.

1. Sit in a comfortable meditation posture. Feel your sitting bones rooted solidly. Sit up with a steady spine, without trying to straighten out the natural curves. Make sure that the top of your head is parallel to the ceiling, with the back of your neck long.
2. Take a deep inhale, and let out a long exhale. Take two more deep breaths, making the exhale longer than the inhale.
3. Close your eyes and bring your hands into prayer position at the Anahata (heart) chakra.
4. As you breathe in, imagine the syllable "So," and as you breathe out, imagine the syllable "Hum."
5. Do this several times. As you do this, make sure your jaw is relaxed. Begin to feel your entire body relaxing into this mantra.

The Healing Power of Mantras

When you chant or hear chants in Sanskrit, even if you don't know the meaning of the phrases you will receive healing benefits. The vibrations of the syllables produce healing. So chant slowly, listen attentively, and become aware of how the vibration feels. Let it affect you.

BRING YOURSELF INTO ALIGNMENT

One way of taking care of the inevitable stresses and strains on your body and mind that accumulate during the day is to perform this yoga stance, called *Tadasana*.

1. Place your feet hip distance apart, and turn the toes in slightly to keep the broadness of your lower back. Keep your arms at your sides.
2. Create your yoga feet by spreading the toes and balls of the feet, pressing into the big and little toe mounds, and the center of the heel.
3. Bring the weight a little more into the heels. Lift your arches as you ground the feet. Enhance this action by lengthening your leg muscles all the way up to your hips.
4. Lift the top of the kneecaps up by contracting the quadriceps muscle. Firm the muscles of the thigh to the bone. Now you have created a strong and stable base from which the torso will be able to extend.
5. Place you hands on your hips and lift the sides of the body from your hips to your armpits. This action creates length and space in the spine.
6. Bring your arms back to your sides without losing the lift of the spine, and lengthen up through the crown of your head. Try to balance your head over the pelvis.
7. Make sure your shoulders are relaxed and are not riding up to the ears. Press your shoulder blades into your back. Lift and broaden your chest. Breathe, remaining aware of how it feels to be in alignment.

CENTER YOUR BODY

This is a good exercise to do before more rigorous yoga poses or other physical activity. It's also a good way during the day of finding a moment of tranquility.

1. Sit in a comfortable, seated position with your legs crossed. This posture is *Sukasana*.
2. Place a cushion or a folded blanket under your sitz bones (sitting bones); this helps you sit up tall while maintaining the natural curves in your spine.
3. Gently place your hands in your lap. Close your eyes. Relax your forehead, eyes, jaw, and tongue.
4. Scan all the way down your body, relaxing each body part, as you breathe in and out naturally.
5. After scanning the body, simply watch the breath as it flows in and out. Do this for a few breaths.
6. Begin Dirgha breathing. Allow the belly, ribs, and chest to expand in three dimensions as you inhale. As you exhale, allow the chest, ribs, and belly to relax.
7. Continue Dirgha breathing for several breaths. Then, return to the natural breath, and open your eyes.

exercise 65

FIND PEACE AT THE CENTER

This simple exercise focuses on your physical center, your abdominal region. But the relief you find from it (improved digestion and elimination) extends to your spiritual side as well.

1. Stand with your feet parallel, hip-width apart.
2. Balance your weight evenly on your feet and firm them into the floor.
3. Stand tall by lifting the crown of your head up toward the ceiling. Inhale and float your arms up and overhead, with palms turned in and your fingers reaching up.
4. Exhale and draw your navel in and up as you fold forward from the hips, letting your knees bend slightly and your arms sweep down toward the floor and behind you.
5. Ground through your heels and lift your sitting bones toward the ceiling.
6. On an inhale, sweep back up to standing as you lengthen the front of your torso, reaching your arms up and overhead.
7. Repeat the movement five to ten times.
8. Create a steady rhythm as you move with your breath, contracting your abdominals each time that you fold forward. Then return to standing.
9. Pause and take several breaths in stillness, feeling energy circulating through your body.

BALANCE YOUR THROAT CHAKRA

The fifth chakra, you may remember, is the Vishuddha or throat chakra. This is a good exercise if you've been speaking a lot and want to refresh your vocal chords. It uses Lion's Breath, from Exercise 47.

1. Pose on all fours, on your hands and knees. In this position, do three rounds of Lion's Breath. To do this, face forward. Inhale, and give a forceful, long exhale as you open your mouth, stick your tongue out and down, and roll your eyes upward.

2. When you've run out of air, release your facial expression to normal. Then, inhale, then do Lion's Breath again.

3. Gently sit back into a simple cross-legged position with your hands in your lap. Use a cushion under your sitz bones, and if your knees are higher than your hips, place cushions or blocks under your thighs to support them.

4. Gently drop your chin down to your chest, and breathe seven deep breaths in this position. Inhale, and on the exhale gently roll your head to the right so that your right ear is near your right shoulder.

5. Inhale and exhale a few times in this position. On an exhale gently roll your chin back toward the center of your chest, and then over to the left. Inhale and exhale a few times in this position. Bring your head back up into a neutral position. Pause.

6. While looking in front of you do the shell mudra: Hold your left hand so that the fingers are pointing toward the sky and facing to the right. With the fingers of your right hand, hold your left

thumb. As you do this, touch the left middle finger with your right thumb.

7. Hold this shell mudra in front of your chest. Inhale and exhale seven times. Chant the seed mantra for this chakra: *ham*, on the exhale each time. This will help strengthen the throat chakra.

exercise 67

PUSH ENERGY UPWARD

This pose, called the Reverse Table, stimulates upward movement of energy to clear the lungs. It also stretches the entire front of the body to increase the flow of energy. Avoid this pose if you have wrist, shoulder, or neck issues.

1. For this pose, return to the breathing pattern of strong, long exhalations, pausing for a moment or two at the end of each exhale.
2. Sit on the floor with your knees bent, feet hip-distance apart and flat on the floor. Position your heels twelve inches away from your buttocks. Press your palms to the floor behind your hips, shoulder-width apart.
3. With your fingers spread wide, tuck your chin toward your chest. Draw your shoulders back and lift your chest as you inhale deeply.
4. On a long exhalation, press into your feet and hands and lift your hips, thighs, and torso parallel to the floor.
5. Pause with your breath held out for a moment as you draw your navel in toward your spine and up toward your heart. Keep the hips lifted and the chest open.
6. On an inhalation release your buttocks to the floor. Repeat five to ten times then release the pose and pause for several breaths.

exercise 68

BE PRESENT

Among the most powerful concepts of Zen Buddhism is the idea of sitting. Just sitting with *nothing* else added. When nothing is added, you experience your enlightened nature. Most of the time, your mind will be active with thoughts and images. It may get swept away by emotions and stories. Your job is not to get rid of thoughts but to come back. You are learning to be present in the moment.

1. Try to sit still. Do not move. This may seem impossible at first, but the more you move, the more you will want to move. This will require working through discomfort and even pain. Zen is a hard path in this way because it has such a strong emphasis on form. You will learn a lot about yourself by doing so. Sometimes the physical pain can be quite powerful. Sometimes you'll be moving just out of habit. You will see how you wiggle around to get away from the moment.
2. Sit as still as a mountain. *Be* a mountain.

STRETCH FOR OPENNESS

The following yoga exercise, called the Standing Marichyasana, can relieve pressure on the sciatic nerve. It's also good for keeping your muscles toned and your body centered and relaxed. Move through the exercise slowly and with awareness.

1. Place a stool next to the wall. Stand behind it with the left side of your body next to the wall.
2. Put your left foot on the stool with your knee bent to slightly higher than 90 degrees. The left foot should be in line with or slightly higher than the left hip.
3. You can put a wooden block or a book under your right heel to elevate it. The right foot is facing the stool with the toes pointing straight ahead.
4. Inhale and lengthen the spine. Exhale and turn your body toward the wall, placing the fingertips of each hand on the wall at shoulder height but wider apart than the shoulders.
5. As you continue inhaling and lengthening, exhaling and revolving toward the wall, see if you can have your shoulders and chest parallel to the wall.
6. After several breaths in this position, slowly unwind and release. Repeat on the other side of the body.

DEEPEN YOUR MINDFULNESS

There are many ways to practice mindfulness. The more you practice being mindful, the more often you will start to live that way, sometimes without consciously thinking about doing it. Here's an exercise you can do as often as you like. You can take mindfulness breaks like this throughout your day; however, you don't have to take a break to practice mindfulness. You can bring mindfulness to any activity. It simply means being present with what is and being intentional about what you're doing. It might sound simple, and in fact it's surprising how often the mind isn't on what's happening right in the present moment.

1. When you can remember, at any point in your day, stop what you are doing for a moment.
2. With your eyes closed, deepen your breath, and send your awareness to the various parts of your body starting with the top of your head and moving downward to the feet.
3. As you send awareness to each body part, inhale and imagine sending prana (life force energy) to that body part. Exhale, and imagine releasing stress.
4. After you've brought your awareness down to the feet, notice if anywhere in the body you feel discomfort. Make small movements of the body to release tension and stiffness.
5. Finally, take a few very deep inhalations and exhalations. On the final exhale, bring a small smile to your lips.
6. Open your eyes and take another moment to appreciate that small break.

VISUALIZE YOUR CHAKRAS

Visualizing the color associated with each chakra is one way to energize that chakra. The colors typically affect chakras with the following pairings:

* Root chakra and the color red
* Sacral chakra and the color orange
* Solar plexus chakra and the color yellow
* Heart chakra and the color green
* Throat chakra and the color blue
* Third eye chakra and the color indigo
* Crown chakra and the colors white, purple, or gold

The order of these colors corresponds to the colors of the visible rainbow from bottom to top. When you would like to bring energy to a particular chakra, envision the corresponding color glowing brightly in the area of that chakra. Try this visualization:

1. Sit with your sitting bones rooted into the chair or earth.
2. Elongate the spine so you are sitting up straight, and the crown of your head is pointing toward the ceiling.
3. Relax the jaw, relax the arms, relax the belly.
4. Deepen your inhalations and exhalations.
5. On an inhale, envision drawing the color red in through your nostrils and way down deep into the perineum.
6. On the exhale, exhale slowly, imagining any muddy color leaving the body.

7. Repeat this two more times, envisioning the color red going into the region of the perineum.
8. Do this same visualization at each chakra, with its corresponding color. Inhale that color deep into the appropriate area, and exhale any unwanted energy.
9. When you get to the crown chakra, on your final exhale, return to normal breathing.
10. Breathe normally for a few moments, noticing the effects of the visualization. Then, open your eyes.

exercise 72

DRAW ON THE POWER OF ANIMALS

An activity that can help you connect to the earth and water elements in nature is to take a walk, and to be conscious of bringing your senses to the experience. In other words, don't think of all the to-dos and worries while you're on the walk. Allow your mind to relax, and drop into the sensory experiences of the outdoors.

Look for Animals

1. Go to a park, where you're bound to find trees, bushes, and rocks.
2. Take a walk through the park, and walk slowly enough that you can be on the lookout for animals.
3. Listen for sounds, stand still, and see what you can find inside trees and bushes.
4. Bring your eyes to the ground, looking for the animals who scurry on land.
5. If you don't see or hear any animals on your walk, listen for other sounds. Listen for wind in the trees, running water, or rustling in the bushes. Allow your senses to help you connect to nature.
6. Now take in the scents. Notice what you can smell in trees, flowers, and the air: notice where there is fragrance. If it's the appropriate time of year, combine this walk with berry picking. Then you can also taste the wonders of nature.

exercise 73

FIND THE CALM CENTER

Mobility and speed steadily increase in our day-to-day world; most of the technology we take for granted would have been unthinkable a few generations ago. But it can also mean we need to do something extra to feel grounded and calm. Here's something you can fix for yourself that will help.

1. Pour ½ cup almond milk and ½ cup spring water into a pot on the stove.
2. Add a pinch of nutmeg.
3. Add a pinch of unrefined brown sugar.
4. Heat until warm, stirring occasionally.
5. Pour into a mug, and slowly enjoy.

CALM YOUR PITTA

One of the qualities of the dosha pitta is to spread. Pitta types are interested in knowledge and will want to spread what they've learned. A pitta type may be a teacher, a lawyer, or a public figure. So it's not surprising that pitta energy will spread to the nearby chakras, causing them to be excessive. Try this visualization to help calm pitta and cool down:

1. Sit in a comfortable posture for pranayama.
2. Close your eyes.
3. Begin Dirgha pranayama. (See Exercise 39, Practice the Power of Breath, but sit instead of lying down.)
4. Do a few moments of Shitali breathing (see Exercise 40, Take a Cooling Breath), and envision cooling waves as you hear your breath flow in and out.
5. Release Shitali breath, return to Dirgha breath, and continue the visualization of blue, calm waves for several breaths. Blue is a cool color.
6. As you take slow, deep inhalations and exhalations, begin to gently massage the top of your head. Gently and lovingly give yourself a soft head massage. Imagine the crown chakra glowing a soft white, like the shine of a pearl.
7. Slowly and carefully, wipe down your energy field, carrying this pearl-colored light down your entire body. To begin this, hold your hands an inch or two in front of your face and sweep gently in a downward motion, dusting off any turbulent energy as a soft white glow emanates from your hands.

8. Continue this over your whole body, slowly as though you are wiping away cobwebs from your torso and limbs. As you brush each area, visualize pearly white healing energy emanating from your hands. Gently clear your energy field, and send cooling energy into it.

9. After you've wiped head to toe, release control of your breath. Allow your breath to flow naturally.

10. Sit quietly for a few moments. Notice any difference in how you feel.

As you clear your energy field with this gentle sweeping downward motion, you initiate a grounded, stable, and calm state. Ground your energy as though you were a lightning rod, giving your fiery energy to the earth.

MASSAGE YOUR DIGESTION

Take a moment during the day—especially after a meal—to relax and allow your digestive system to work. Drink warm water. The Ayurvedic herbal formula triphala will help your bowels move. Other natural remedies are to eat prunes, take a relaxing walk, and try a wind-relieving pose.

1. Lie on your back with your legs straight out on the floor.
2. Take a few deep breaths, and relax into the support of the earth.
3. Bend your right knee and draw it up to your chest as far as is comfortable. Keep the left leg straight on the ground. Use both hands to hold the right knee into your chest. Breathe deeply several times, feeling your belly rise up against your right thigh.
4. On an exhale, straighten the right leg back onto the floor.
5. Repeat steps two through four, using the left leg.
6. Gently roll over onto your left side. Then, slowly get up.

MAKE SPACE FOR
NEW BEGINNINGS

As you heal your chakras, you will be eliminating what you don't want to carry around with you anymore—physically, psychologically, and energetically. How much are you ready to release? When you exhale, when you sweat, and when you go to the bathroom, you are releasing. These are examples of how your body eliminates waste including emotions, food, and energy that you no longer want or need. There is a hand mudra that can help this process, the apana mudra:

1. Hold your hands out so that the palms face up.
2. Curl the ring finger and middle finger of each hand to touch the fingertip of the thumb of the same hand.
3. Hold this posture for fifteen minutes, three times per day.

CHANT TO YOUR CHAKRAS

Your chakras will respond to sound, particularly to the sound of you chanting. For this exercise, choose the chakra you want to affect and chant the sound that is associated with it:

* O as in OM for the root
* OO as in POOL for the sacral
* AH as in DHARMA for the solar plexus
* A as in SPACE for the heart
* E as in FREE for the throat
* MM as in MEDIUM for the third eye
* NNG as in WING for the crown

Chant the appropriate sound while sitting calmly, mindful of your breathing, concentrating on the sound and on feeling it surge through the associated chakra.

exercise 78

CHANT A MANTRA WITH EACH CHAKRA

There's a particular *bija* or seed mantra associated with each chakra. It is said that by chanting the bija mantra that corresponds to each chakra, you connect with the essence of that energy center. Visualize each chakra and repeat the associated bija mantra, shown in the following table.

Bija Mantras and Corresponding Chakras

BIJA MANTRA	CHAKRA
Lam	Root
Vam	Sacral
Ram	Solar Plexus
Yam	Heart
Ham	Throat
Om or Ksham	Third Eye
Om or Silence	Crown

Like several things with chakra healing, not all healers agree on the same bija mantras. Chakra healing is both rooted in history and also experiential because each person is unique. Test them out, and see which resonates with you best.

WRITE IN A REIKI JOURNAL

For this, get an actual notebook, binder, or journal. You'll find that the physical act of writing, even if it's only a few sentences a day, is liberating in a way that typing on your computer's keyboard isn't.

1. Write a couple of pages about yourself and your reasons for practicing Reiki.
2. Write about what Reiki is doing to your life. Don't worry if you're rambling or off the subject. This is a private forum in which you can express any thoughts without judgment or fear.
3. Make an intention statement. State your intention as clearly and concisely as possible so it can't be misunderstood. Follow that intention statement with a brief dedication.
4. Bless your journal by holding it between both of your hands and allowing Reiki energies to flow freely from your palms into its pages.

GIVE YOURSELF A BEDTIME MASSAGE

If you have trouble falling asleep (and even if you don't and just want to promote a deep, uninterrupted sleep), give yourself a massage before going to bed.

1. Heat sesame oil for the vata and kapha body types, or coconut oil for the pitta types, until it's warm to the touch.
2. With slow, soothing strokes, massage your feet with the warm oil.
3. Wash your hands and cover your feet with socks do you don't stain your bedsheets with oil.
4. Massage warm oil along the brow line and at the crown of your head as you take deep, soothing breaths.

BE A WARRIOR

This yoga pose, Virabhadrasana 1, is warrior pose, a vigorous posture that provides a tremendous stretch to the torso, the spine, and the back leg.

1. Stand with your arms by your sides. Jump or walk the legs four feet apart. Extend your arms to the sides, palms facing up. Stretch into the fingertips and feel the opening of the chest and ribs. Inhale and lift your arms over your head.

2. Connect the stretch of the side ribs with the lifting of the arms. Keep the palms facing each other, lengthen the arms, and firm the elbows. If the elbows bend, bring the arms wider apart, in the shape of a V. By straightening the elbows, you will enhance the lifting of the side ribs and the extension of the spine.

3. Turn the left foot in (45 to 60 degrees) and revolve the right leg out. On an exhalation, turn your body to face the right (front) leg. Ground through the feet, lift the arches, and extend all the way from the feet to the legs, the side body, and the fingertips. Relax the top of the shoulders away from the ears to maintain the length of the neck and to release shoulder tension. Keep the eyes, face, and throat soft.

4. Inhale the breath for extension, and as you exhale, bend the right leg (knee over ankle) and lengthen the left leg, pressing the top of the left thigh back.

5. Lengthen the left leg from the hip to the heel. Bend the right leg, with the intention of creating a right angle. Continue to stretch from the side ribs into the fingertips to maintain lift and extension in the body. Stay for a few breaths.

6. Come out of the pose by pressing the feet firmly into the floor, carefully lengthening the front leg, turning the feet to parallel, facing center, bringing the arms down, and jumping the feet back to Tadasana (see Exercise 63). Repeat on the other side.

LOOK BACK ON YOUR DAY

Take a few minutes at the end of the day to remember what you've done and how you've felt. Write down the following questions on a piece of paper, one at a time, and answer them:

1. What did I do right after I woke up this morning?
2. How was I feeling when I woke up this morning?
3. Was I rushing around this morning, running late, or wondering how I'd be able to squeeze everything into the day?
4. Did I make time to eat? How many meals? How did I feel when eating?
5. Did I find time for myself, to take a pause, breathe, or laugh?
6. How am I feeling right now?

BREATHE OUT TENSION

When you are anxious, your energy is predominantly up in your mind. Although high energy is certainly an asset in many situations, here we want to bring it down so you can relax and let go of your anxiety.

1. Go outside, if possible, to allow the earth's force to help ground you.
2. Breathe in and out slowly, gently, and deeply.
3. Feel your body expand to allow the air to rush inward on the inhale.
4. Envision your connection to the earth as you imagine your inhale going through your body to the ground.
5. Create a longer exhalation than inhalation to induce relaxation. Imagine the energy coming down from your head out through the Muladhara chakra into the earth.
6. After several minutes, take a final cleansing breath and relax.

STAND AND MEDITATE

Take some breaks from work, if you can. Take a tea break, find time for a nap, or take a walk outside and feel the grounding energy of the earth. Here is a standing meditation you can do at any time of day, to help you feel grounded.

Standing Meditation

1. Stand with feet parallel, hip-width apart.
2. Spread the toes and press evenly and firmly down through the four corners of each foot.
3. Release the tailbone down while lifting the sternum and crown of the head up. Stand tall with the arms by the sides, shoulders relaxed.
4. Relax the muscles in the face, shoulders, and belly.
5. Seal the lips and begin to breathe, slow and steady, through the nostrils. Draw deep breaths in and out.
6. With your feet hip-width apart, turn the toes in and heels out just a bit, so the feet are slightly pigeon-toed.
7. Exhale and bend the knees slightly. Let the shin bones move forward then drop down into the force of gravity. Balance the weight evenly on the heels and balls of the feet then let them sink into the earth.
8. Soften the gaze. Place both hands on the belly, and relax the belly and all of its contents.
9. Relax the muscles in the thighs and buttocks. Use as little muscular effort as possible. Let the bones support you. Feel the bones becoming heavy and surrender their weight to gravity.

10. Let yourself sink into the stance. Soften the muscles in the legs and sink into the support of the bones. Allow yourself to connect to the strength and support they have to offer.

11. To release, bring the feet back to parallel, inhale, and sweep the arms to the sides and overhead as the legs straighten. Press the palms together and exhale them down to prayer position at the heart. Take a deep breath in and let out an audible sigh.

Pause and feel the echo of the meditation in the mind and body, tuning in to what is present. Enjoy this standing mediation anytime you need to experience grounding and stability in your life.

DO A MINDFULNESS EXERCISE

A meditation exercise in mindfulness meditation usually starts by focusing on the physical body and then moving to the mind.

1. Start by using a technique of "scanning" or "sweeping" the body from bottom to top. Start with the feet; move up in sequence to the calves, thighs, torso, arms, neck, and head.
2. Move your focus slowly. With eyes closed, train your attention on each section of your body. Note the sensations of heat and cold, the air on your skin, the texture of the muscles, any stiffness, any pulsing sensations. Give yourself ten minutes for this.
3. When you have finished with your head, move your attention to breathing. Note its evenness and rhythm. Give yourself five minutes for this.
4. Now relax your attention and observe your thoughts. If thinking interferes with observing, go back to scanning your body.

exercise 86

SAY A NATIVE AMERICAN PRAYER

Although separated by vast regions of geography and climate, all Native Americans shared the belief that the creative spirit could be accessed through nature. The key to achieving that was experiencing and living in harmony with natural forces. There were many ways of pursuing this goal: by carefully observing animals, weather patterns, and the elements of wind, sun, and moon. Through observing, Native Americans believed that the spirit of those things could communicate with human beings and enlarge their understanding. These efforts were not seen as tasks or methods to be learned. Rather, they were viewed as extended meditations, or living meditatively.

Here's a Cheyenne prayer that you can say to yourself to gain a quiet moment of inspiration:

Let us know peace.
For as long as the Moon shall rise,
For as long as rivers shall flow,
For as long as the Sun will shine,
For as long as the grass shall grow,
Let us know peace.

ENGAGE IN CREATIVE VISUALIZATION

Creative visualization engages your imagination. In the middle of a busy day, it can be helpful to take a moment to daydream, as you do in this meditation. Note that this script isn't the only possible one; take some time and write down other scripts that you find calming and peaceful and use them in your meditations.

1. Take a deep breath, exhaling peacefully. Closing your eyes, feel warmth surrounding you like a cocoon. It is protective and secure, assuring you that your rest will not be disturbed.
2. See yourself walking down a familiar hallway, carpeted with a beautiful, luxuriant rug. Two glass doors are at the end of the hallway, and as you get closer to them, you see a large, inviting room.
3. Standing before the glass doors, you look inside. The room is a library, filled with books. They are all bound beautifully, in brilliant colors with gold-stamped titles. You want to go inside and see these books, touch them, read them. You grasp the brass handle of one of the doors, open it and go inside.
4. The room is hushed and peaceful. The scent of sandalwood fills the air. The light in the room is bright but gentle, allowing you to see all around. There are comfortable chairs and footrests before the richly stained wooden bookshelves.
5. You go up to one of the bookshelves. Handsomely bound volumes are neatly stacked together. You pick out a book, one that is not too large or small, but fits well in your hand. You open the book and begin to turn the pages and read.

6. After you have studied the contents of this book to your satisfaction, you place it back on the shelf and stand back. You glance around at other books on other shelves, looking forward to the next time you can choose a new volume to examine.

7. You leave the room, closing the glass door behind you and looking in the library for a moment. It was a good visit, and one that will be repeated many times to come. You walk confidently back down the hallway, back to your meditation oasis, where you are in your warm cocoon.

8. Slowly you return to everyday consciousness. You are calm and relaxed, at complete rest on the outside and the inside. Ask yourself what you read in the book.

exercise 88

PERFORM A NIGHTTIME VISUALIZATION

Visualizations are a wonderful way to calm down after a long day. At the very least, if you cannot make a lot of time to slow down before bed, try this visualization either in a comfortable chair before bed or once you are lying in bed.

1. Get comfortable, and close your eyes.
2. Notice yourself sinking into the support of the bed. Take a moment and a few deep breaths to sink into that support.
3. Bring a slight smile to your lips. This will trigger a happy and peaceful feeling.
4. Envision yourself lying down underneath a blue sky.
5. Notice there are just a few clouds, and watch them float slowly across the sky.
6. Envision all the tension melting from your body, sinking down through the bed, down into the earth, melting away. Return your imagination to the blue sky, and your breath.

exercise 89

TRY PARTNER YOGA

A fun way to practice yoga in the family is to try partner yoga poses. Partner yoga helps build connection between two people, and it's fun. When you are in a partner yoga posture, you and your partner are practicing communication. You'll ease into postures together, hold, and then help each other release the posture. You can communicate both with your voices and also with the energy of the body.

1. Stand with your partner shoulder to shoulder, facing the same direction, holding hands, with your inside feet touching.
2. Each take a big step to the side with the outer foot, turning that foot out 90 degrees.
3. Keep a good, strong hold, and bend the outer leg, sending the knee in the direction of the middle toe. The outside arms lift to shoulder height and reach out in the same direction as the foot. Head turns to look over the outstretched hand.
4. Check in with your partner. Make adjustments for special needs and for comfort.
5. Hold for three or four breaths. Explore this pose with great support; experiment by sinking deeper into it.
6. When you are ready, tell each other, and gently release the pose by bringing yourself back to the starting position.
7. Thank your partner, and change positions. Repeat on the other side.

DO A HULA HOOP VISUALIZATION

Here's another imaginative visualization you can try.

1. Imagine a large Hula Hoop floating horizontally in the air above you. The hoop represents a vortex opening into a different reality.
2. Visualize the Reiki power symbol, Cho Ku Rei, floating inside the circular hoop.
3. Next, imagine yourself jumping up into the hoop and through the power symbol into a new reality of your making. This reality can be a revisitation to your childhood, a swim date with a school of dolphins, or an explorative tour through an enchanted castle.
4. Now relax and come back to full consciousness. With the help of this visualization, you can go virtually anywhere your mind will take you.

Cho Ku Rei

The first Reiki symbol, Cho Ku Rei, is the power symbol. It is a spiral-shaped symbol that is often referred to as "the light switch." You can see an image of it here: *www.reikirays.com/86/cho-ku-rei*. The Cho Ku Rei symbol represents the engine that gives Reiki its initial boost. Whenever Reiki needs a nudge to get started or there is a need for an increase in power when applying Reiki, this symbol can be used. In absentia treatments, the Cho Ku Rei serves as the delivery system.

CALM ANXIETY

Anxiety can be relieved by calming down vata. To counteract excess vata, which makes you dry and cold, find ways to bring heat and moisture to your body. Here's an exercise to bring your focus to all your chakras; this will help calm vata.

1. Start your visualization at the root chakra. Imagine the root chakra glowing bright red. Feel your sitting bones stable, supported by the earth. Inhale and exhale with your attention at the root.
2. Place your hands one on top of the other on your torso at the location of the sacral chakra. Notice how your own hands on your body are grounding, comforting. Hold your hands at the area where the sacral chakra blossoms, and imagine a bright orange color as you inhale and exhale.
3. Move your hands up to the solar plexus. Imagine the bright yellow glow of your third chakra.
4. Continue this up your body at the heart, throat, and third eye chakras.
5. Finally, place your hands on top of your head at the crown. Through your hands, visualize calming, healing white light flooding your brain through this chakra. Visualize yourself relaxed.
6. Release your hands. Take a moment, notice if there have been any changes in how you feel. Notice your breath, your level of physical tension, and your mind.

exercise 92

FOCUS ON SELF-CARE

If you have habits you'd like to stop (smoking, drinking, watching too much TV, and so forth), you need to focus your attention on self-care. Try the following meditation when you feel the urge to indulge in your bad habit.

1. Sit in a comfortable position for meditation, with your sitting bones firmly planted on the chair, or on a cushion if you are on the floor. Sit upright, allow the natural curves of the spine to be as they are. Make sure the top of your head is parallel to the ceiling. Gently rest your hands in your lap.
2. After you've read all the following steps, then close your eyes to do them.
3. Relax your jaw, and all the muscles of your face. From top to bottom notice each body part and relax it. Relax the forehead, the jaw, the neck, the shoulders, the arms, the hands, the torso, the belly, the hips, the thighs, the calves, the ankles, and the toes.
4. Breathe naturally for several breaths, and notice the breath as it flows in and as it flows out. Watch and observe how your torso expands on the inhale, and lets go on the exhale.
5. Now with your eyes closed, do a chakra scan: at each chakra envision its corresponding color glowing. Start at the crown chakra. Envision it glowing white, and notice how it and you respond. Relax for several breaths, and notice.
6. Draw your attention down to each chakra, envisioning the color of the chakra for several breaths. Noticing how you feel.

7. After you've done this at the root chakra, continue to observe the breath for a few moments.
8. Place both of your hands on your body over your heart. Position your hands either in prayer position with the side of the hands touching, or with one hand on top of the other facing your heart. Imagine your hands giving your heart energy; loving, restoring energy.
9. When you feel complete, release your hands, and open your eyes.

MAKE CHOICES FROM A PLACE OF LOVE

According to the Law of Attraction, if you have resistant thoughts to what you desire, you are blocking what you want from coming to you. Taking time in your life to practice chakra healing and getting used to keeping in mind the Law of Attraction is a perfect combination to creating the conditions to allow the natural flow of energy. To use chakra healing and the law of attraction to help cultivate fearlessness, buy a clear quartz or amethyst crystal that you can hold in the palms of your hands. It will support your crown chakra for this exercise.

1. Have the crystal nearby, but not yet in your hands.
2. Take a moment to bring to mind one big thing that your heart desires. Allow your mind to go to what fears you may have around receiving this next thing. If you want, write the fears down, now. Then, place the paper to the side.
3. Pick up the crystal, and hold it inside your cupped hands: one hand on top of the other, with the crystal inside.
4. Feel the energy of the crystal in your hands. Feel the energy travel through your arms, into your entire body, cleansing your body of doubt, fear, or anxiety. If you don't feel it, it's okay. Visualize it.
5. Breathe in and out naturally for several breaths while envisioning the pure, vibrant energy replacing insecurities held in your body and mind.

6. Put the crystal down, and on a new piece of paper write down how you are feeling now. Notice if there have been any positive shifts in your energy.

7. Throw away or burn the piece of paper with your fears on it.

Practice Removing Obstacles

In the *Yoga Sutras* of Patanjali, he explains that there is a natural evolution and flow, and the purpose of practice is to remove obstacles that are in the way. Sutra 4.3: "incidental events do not directly cause natural evolution, they just remove the obstacles as a farmer removes the obstacles in a water course running to his field."

LET IT GO

No, not the song from *Frozen*. But sometimes when you want to let go and allow things to take their course, strengthening any and all of the chakras always helps. Specifically, if you are feeling insecure, it can be mainly in the solar plexus chakra. If you are feeling insecure, try this exercise.

1. Sit in a position for meditation.
2. Place your hands one on top of the other on your solar plexus.
3. Practice Kapalabhati breath (see Exercises 13 and 46). If you are new to it, just practice ten exhales. If you are used to it, do thirty. Relax, then repeat two more times.
4. Notice how you feel.
5. Keeping your hands where they are, and while breathing normally, envision glowing yellow light emanating from your hands into your third chakra. Do this for several moments.
6. When you are done with this visualization, take a moment to come back to the present moment.

REMOVE FEAR

If you are afraid or worried about something, you can get help from the Muladhara (root) chakra. When you are anxious, your mind will spin in circles of worry. You also might notice physical effects: your heart may beat faster, your breath may become shallow, and your belly may become upset. Chronic anxiety can lead to various physical symptoms and disease.

When you are anxious, your energy is predominantly up in your mind. So, you want to bring your energy down. Doing something physical, energizing the body, will bring energy down from the mind into the body.

1. If the weather permits, get outside to allow the earth's force to help ground you.
2. Whether or not you can get outside, breathe in and out slowly, gently, and deeply, feeling your body expand to allow the air to rush inward on the inhale.
3. Envision your connection to the earth; imagine your inhale going through your body into the ground. Create longer exhalation than inhalation to induce relaxation.
4. If you are standing up, imagine your legs as though they have roots growing deeply into the earth. Know you are rooted and connected. If you want to sit down on the ground or floor, then you can imagine the energy coming down from your head out through the Muladhara chakra into the earth.
5. For several minutes, breathe and envision energy coming down into the body and flowing into the earth.

PRANAYAMA FOR CENTEREDNESS

Pranayama, or breathing, is central to many of the disciplines in this book. It's a powerful, ancient way of directing energy in the body. Be creative about when and where you practice pranayama to bring more health and vitality into your life. This exercise uses *Anuloma Viloma* to help you center yourself.

1. Sit in a comfortable seated position.
2. Practice Nadi Shodhana (alternate nostril breathing; see Exercise 11) for a few rounds.
3. To start Anuloma Viloma, retain the breath for a few seconds between the inhale and the exhale.
4. As you get more comfortable, hold the breath longer between the inhale and exhale, and just observe what happens in your body.
5. Repeat the cycles of Anuloma Viloma for up to fifteen minutes to receive the balancing benefits of the practice. Then, after you are finished, pause and notice the effects.

exercise 97

REVITALIZE YOUR BODY

The following exercise is based on the meditative exercises of the Taoist path and is called Embryonic Breathing. Imagine your body is divided into three zones, called cinnabar fields. The lower cinnabar field extends from your navel down to your feet. The middle cinnabar field is your chest, and the upper cinnabar field is the brain.

1. Begin in standing position.
2. Take in three normal breaths, being very conscious of them.
3. With the fourth breath, take it in and pause for a moment.
4. In this brief pause, see the air vitalize the lower cinnabar field. It goes through your nose to the navel, and it continues downward to your feet. Release the breath.
5. With the fifth breath, take it in and pause for a moment.
6. In this brief pause, see the air vitalize the middle cinnabar field. It goes from your nose to your spine. Release the breath.
7. With the sixth breath, take it in and pause for a moment.
8. In this brief pause, see the air vitalize the upper cinnabar field. It goes from your nose upward to the crown of your head.
9. Relax and breathe normally.

TAKE A ZEN TEA BREAK

The Japanese tea ceremony Cha-no Yu ("water for tea") was originally devised to prevent monks from falling asleep during deep meditation exercise. Gradually, the discipline itself became a ritualized ceremony, providing an opportunity for the contemplation of timeless images. For this exercise, use powdered or loose green tea and a teapot.

1. Start the fire. (If you're not a monk preparing your tea in a strictly traditional fashion, either turn on the stove element or plug in the kettle.)
2. Pour the water slowly and deliberately into the heating container and place it on the fire.
3. Watch the water as it heats. When it comes to a rolling boil, remove it from the fire and scoop the tea into it. Cover and allow it to steep for a few minutes.
4. Pour the tea into the teapot, using the strainer.
5. Pour the tea into a cup.
6. Pick up the cup with your right hand and place it in the left hand, with the fingers of the right hand still around the cup. Your thumb should be facing you. Make a small, polite bow.
7. Now, turn the bowl clockwise 90 degrees with the thumb and forefinger of your right hand. Take a sip, and allow the fragrance of the tea to rise up to your nose.
8. Continue drinking the tea in small sips. When you are finished, inhale deeply and audibly.
9. Turn the cup counterclockwise 90 degrees with the thumb and forefinger back to its original position when you picked it up.

The Tea Drinking Ceremony

Although the tea ceremony is a group meditation, you may observe it on your own, as shown above. A separate space is ideal for this, where fresh flowers, a tidy table, and a comfortable chair can be placed. Traditionally, the ceremony is held in the teahouse, with the participants sitting on the floor on a tatami mat and cushions. The ceremony is quite elaborate, and dictated by a protocol that covers every possible detail. The manner of entering the room, sitting, and speaking are outlined with guidelines of simplicity and flawlessness.

SOOTHE WITH SOUP

It's possible that you're standing over a stove, heating some soup for your lunch on a cold winter's day. This is a chance to make this small, everyday task more meaningful with a meditation. Let this event be the only focus of your attention.

1. Listen for the sounds of steam, bubbling liquid, and stirring.
2. Observe the motion of the liquid as it heats and is stirred, watching the ingredients change texture and color.
3. Taste the soup slowly and periodically, noticing changes in flavor and temperature
4. Distinguish the variations in scent as the soup is heated, cooled, and tasted.
5. Before sitting down to eat your lunch, take a long, calming breath and exhale slowly.

FIND BALANCE

Balance is both a physical and a spiritual quality. Just as you learn to balance on your feet as an infant and step forward and backward, so as an adult you have to learn to balance your life and find the calm center. This exercise is helpful in linking these two aspects of balance.

1. Stand upright, feet slightly spaced, with your dominant foot about four inches in front of the other. Balance yourself in this position.
2. Bend the knees slightly and start to rock, forward and backward. Movement should be very slow and deliberate, but do not press your feet into the floor. Your motions should be easy and subtle, as if you are surfing over water.
3. After rocking for two to three minutes, return to an upright standing posture and change your foot position. This time, the opposite foot will be placed in front of the dominant one. Repeat the forward-backward rocking motion with bent knees for two to three minutes.
4. Pay attention to any differences in your sensations of balance. Adjust your body stance accordingly when you repeat the exercise.

TAKE PURIFICATION BREATHS

This exercise prepares you for rhythmic breathing. The breaths are called the five purifications of the soul. The universal elements are the focal points: earth, water, fire, and air.

1. Begin at sunrise, if possible, when the elements are at their peak. Stand upright.
2. Breathe slowly and deeply, keeping in mind the energy of the earth. Visualize it as the color yellow, entering your body as you inhale through the nose. The earth element travels upward from the ground through your spine to your crown. As it does so, the earth filters out all impurities. It returns to the ground when you exhale through the nose. Repeat this four times (a total of five).
3. Breathe slowly and deeply, keeping in mind the energy of water. Visualize it as the color green, entering your nose as you inhale. The water element moves upward from the stomach, through your spine to your crown. As it does so, the liquid washes away all impurities. It exits from your stomach when you exhale through the mouth. Repeat this four times (a total of five).
4. Breathe slowly and deeply, keeping in mind the energy of fire. Visualize it as the color red, entering your body through your heart as you inhale. The fire element moves upward to your crown. As it does so, the fire burns away all impurities. It exits from your heart when you exhale through the nose. Repeat this four times (a total of five).

REPEAT ST. FRANCIS'S PRAYER

In the thirteenth century, despite an early life of privilege and ease, a young Italian named Francesco di Bernardone received a spiritual command through prayer to dedicate his life to peace and contemplation. In answer to this, he was to found the brotherhood of the "little friars." They came to play a significant role in European spirituality in the following centuries as the Franciscans. Their founder was known as St. Francis of Assisi. He wrote the following meditation on peace. Recite it quietly to yourself. If you like, write it out and put it somewhere you'll see it every day.

Lord, make me an instrument of your peace;
Where there is hatred, let me sow love;
Where there is injury, pardon;
Where there is doubt, faith;
Where there is despair, hope;
Where there is darkness, light;
And where there is sadness, joy.
Grant that I may not so much seek to be consoled as to console;
To be understood as to understand,
To be loved as to love.
For it is in giving that we receive,
It is in pardoning that we are pardoned,
And it is in dying that we are born to eternal life.

exercise 103

MOVE YOUR MOOD TO MUSIC

If a more stimulating shift of energy is what you need, bring some dance into your life. Use your favorite CD or DVD (with earbuds, if you don't want to disturb others around you). There isn't a right or wrong way to dance: let the music be your body's guide.

1. If you aren't used to dancing or letting the music inform your movement, try this.
2. When you turn on the music, even if it's fast-paced, close your eyes and pause. Wait a few moments to let the rhythm of the beat and the sounds affect your body; you don't have to think about it.
3. After several moments, allow yourself to move in any way you like. The body knows what it needs; it will inform you.
4. Do it with a light attitude—there's no one judging you. Smile as your body flows through space, and allow your mood to shift.

DO A STANDING WIDE ANGLE FORWARD FOLD

Benefits of this exercise include: the pose cools and circulates abdominal energy; it calms an overheated brain; and it sends excess heat down the energy channels in the legs and into the earth. If you're suffering from lower-back issues, either avoid this pose, or keep your knees bent while practicing it.

1. Stand with your feet three to four feet apart with hands on your hips.
2. Bring your feet parallel to each other and press the outer edges of your feet firmly into the floor.
3. Firm up your thigh muscles.
4. Inhale and lift your chest.
5. Hinging at the hips, exhale and lift your tailbone as you fold forward, keeping your spine long.
6. When your torso is parallel to the floor, place your hands on the floor directly below your shoulders. (Place your hands on blocks or thick books as a modification. Or, if the backs of your legs or spine are tight, bend your knees.)
7. Distribute your weight evenly between your hands and feet. Work to lengthen your arms and legs.
8. Widen your shoulder blades across your back and draw your shoulders away from your ears.
9. Gaze straight down and lengthen your spine from the tip of your tailbone through the crown of your head.
10. Stay in the pose for five to ten deep breaths, with an emphasis on longer exhalations for a cooling effect.

exercise 105

WISH HAPPINESS

Wishing happiness for all beings can take practice. There's a special kind of meditation that is used for cultivating this ability. It's called *metta meditation*. There are variations, but in general this is how you practice metta:

1. Sit in a comfortable, seated position for meditation.
2. Close your eyes, and follow your breath as it goes in and out several times.
3. Say this to yourself: "May I be happy. May I be healthy. May I know peace."
4. Bring to mind someone you love dearly. Hold this person in your mind's eye. Repeat the same wish: "May you be happy. May you be healthy. May you know peace."
5. Bring to mind someone who is an acquaintance whom you have good feelings toward, and don't know very well. Perhaps it's someone who works in the same building as you, or the person at the post office who always helps your mail your packages. Hold this person in your mind's eye, and say: "May you be happy. May you be healthy. May you know peace."
6. Now repeat this for all beings: "May all beings be happy. May all beings be healthy. May all beings know peace." When you are finished, open your eyes.

appendix

REIKI HAND POSITIONS

Knowing the correct positioning of your hands is essential for some of the Reiki-based exercises in this book. Here, we show you how your hands should be positioned to practice Reiki.

YOUR REIKI HANDS

Wash your hands thoroughly before you begin. You may want to remove any rings or bracelets from your fingers and wrists, especially if you are sensitive to the vibrational energies of gold, silver, or gemstones. When you place your hands on your body, be gentle, gentle, gentle! No pressure needs to be applied, since it is the exchange of ki energies that effectively does the healing work for you. When you place your hands, palms facing downward, onto your body, Reiki will begin to flow automatically.

Always begin at the face placement and move downward. Devote five minutes to each placement in order to make sure you don't neglect any part of your body and so that each body part is given equal consideration. Wear a watch or place a clock within your visual range so that you can closely monitor the time spent on each placement.

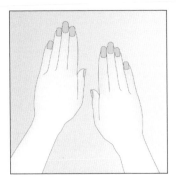

REIKI HANDS

When you use your hands to administer Reiki, hold the fingers and thumbs of each of your hands snugly together so there are no obvious gaps or spaces between them. Remember: All you need is a light touch to get the ki flowing.

PLACEMENT 1: FACE

Place the palms of your hands against the sides of your face, cupping your hands softly over your eyes. Rest the tips of your fingers gently against your forehead. Do not cover your nose and mouth—leave them exposed between your hands. Take care not to squeeze your nostrils, as you do not want to obstruct your breathing. Hold the fingers and thumbs of each of your hands snugly together so there are no obvious gaps or spaces between them.

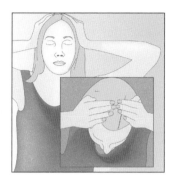

PLACEMENT 2: CROWN AND TOP OF THE HEAD

Take your hands and place the base of each palm just slightly above your ears. Wrap both your palms and fingers along your skull, so that your fingertips meet at the crown.

PLACEMENT 3: BACK OF THE HEAD

Cross your arms behind your head, placing one hand on the back of your head and the other directly below it and just above the nape of your neck.

PLACEMENT 4: CHIN AND JAW LINE

Cup your chin and jaw line in your hands, so that your inner wrists touch beneath your chin. Gently rest your fingertips over your earlobes.

PLACEMENT 5: NECK, COLLARBONE, AND HEART

Place your right hand over the front of your neck, grasping your throat gently while allowing your neck to be held inside the space between your outward-extended thumb and fingers. Rest your left hand on top of your chest, between your collarbone and your heart.

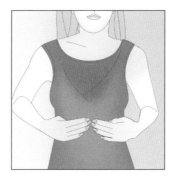

PLACEMENT 6: RIBS

Place your hands on your rib cage, just below your breasts, with your fingertips touching. Your elbows should be bent back a little.

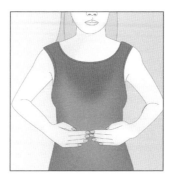

PLACEMENT 7: ABDOMEN

Place your hands on your solar plexus area, just above your navel. Keep your elbows bent and allow your fingertips to touch.

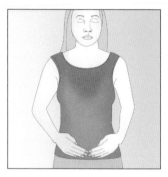

PLACEMENT 8: PELVIC BONES

Place your right hand over your right pelvic bone and place your left hand over your left pelvic bone, so that your fingertips touch in the center.

PLACEMENT 9: SHOULDERS AND SHOULDER BLADES

Reach over the top of your shoulders and place your hands on your shoulder blades. If you cannot reach your shoulder blades, reach only as far as you are able to comfortably. As an option, you can rest your hands on the top of your shoulders.

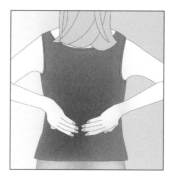

PLACEMENT 10: MIDBACK

Reach behind your back, elbows bent, and place your hands on the middle of your back. Allow your fingertips to touch, if you are able to do so comfortably.

PLACEMENT 11: LOWER BACK

Reach behind your back, elbows bent, and place your hands on your lower back. Allow your fingertips to touch, if you are able to do so comfortably.

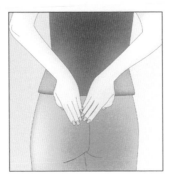

PLACEMENT 12: SACRUM

Reach behind your back, elbows bent, and place your hands on your sacral region.

INDEX